Toilet Roll Covers

PAT ASHFORTH & STEVE PLUMMER

GUILD OF MASTER
CRAFTSMAN PUBLICATIONS

First published 2007 by
Guild of Master Craftsman Publications Ltd
Castle Place, 166 High Street,
Lewes, East Sussex BN7 1XU

Text © Pat Ashforth and Steve Plummer, 2007
Copyright in the Work © GMC Publications Ltd, 2007

ISBN: 978-1-86108-499-6

A catalogue record of this book is available from
the British Library.

Charts by Rebecca Mothersole
Pattern checking by Alison Howard
Knitting and crochet illustrations by Simon Rodway

Managing Editor: Gerrie Purcell
Production Manager: Jim Bulley
Editor: Alison Howard
Managing Art Editor: Gilda Pacitti
Design & Photography: Rebecca Mothersole

Set in Gill Sans and Ribbon

Colour origination by AltaImage
Printed & bound in Thailand by Kyodo Nation Printing Services
under the supervision of MRM Graphics, Winslow, Bucks.

Why we love toilet roll covers

Toilet roll covers are easy, fun and quick to make, and are ideal small gifts. They can be made to suit individual tastes, decor or personal interests – or just make one for yourself! From the sophisticated to the downright silly, all the covers in this book are worked using double-knitting weight yarn. Have fun!

Contents

This easy garter stitch cover can be made in any colour combination, and is perfect for the novice knitter

Simply Stunning

Materials and Equipment

- 65 yards (60 metres) main yarn (M)
- 22 yards (20 metres) contrasl yarn (C)
- Straight needles

Tension

19 stitches should produce a width of approximately 4in (10cm) over garter stitch

Method

Work in garter stitch throughout. The example was worked with a six-armed spiral top, but if this is your first cover, you may find it easier to work a straight top and separate sides. The straight top pattern produces an octagonal shape, with each of the sides equivalent to nine stitches in width. This pulls into a round when the sides are attached. Working the first ridge of the sides in the same colour as the top produces a far neater join. For an eight-armed spiral, see the General Instructions on page 148.

Tops
Straight

Using C, cast on 9 stitches.

Row 1: k to the last stitch; increase in the last stitch.

Repeat this row until there are 23 stitches on the needle.

Work 18 rows.

Next row: k to the last 2 stitches, k2tog.

Repeat this row until there are 10 stitches on the needle.

Cast off loosely, knitting the last two stitches together before casting them off.

Six-armed spiral

Using C, cast on 6 sts.

Row 1: inc in each st (12 sts).

Row 2 and all even-numbered rows: k to end.

Row 3: (inc in next st, k1) to end (18 sts).

Row 5: (inc in next st, k2) to end (24 sts).

Row 7: (inc in next st, k3) to end (30 sts).

Row 9: (inc in next st, k4) to end (36 sts).

Row 11: (inc in next st, k5) to end (42 sts).

Row 13: (inc in next st, k6) to end (48 sts).

Row 15: (inc in next st, k7) to end (54 sts).

Row 17: (inc in next st, k8) to end (60 sts).

Row 19: (inc in next st, k9) to end (66 sts).

Row 21: (inc in next st, k10) to end (72 sts).

Cast off loosely if preferred, or leave these 72 stitches on the needle and continue for the sides.

Sides
For the straight top

Using straight needles and C, cast on 72 stitches.

Work one row.

Break off C. RS facing, join in M.

Work until the cover is long enough to fit the toilet roll.

Cast off.

Alternative method

Using C and straight needles or a circular needle to work back and forth, pick up and knit 9 sts from each of the sides of the straight top (72 stitches).

Turn and work one row.

Break off C. RS facing, join in M.

Work until the cover is long enough to fit the toilet roll.

Cast off.

For the spiral top

Join in M and continue on the 72 stitches left on the needle after working the top.

Work until the cover is long enough to fit the toilet roll.

Cast off.

Finishing

Join the back seam to form a cylinder. Spiral top: join seam neatly following hints for joining garter stitch (see the General Instructions at end of book). Straight top: from the inside, oversew the white edge of the sides to the edges of the top, using 9 cast-on stitches on each side of the octagonal shape.

Variations

- work top and sides in a single colour
- work the sides in stripes
- use a fancy textured yarn for a different effect

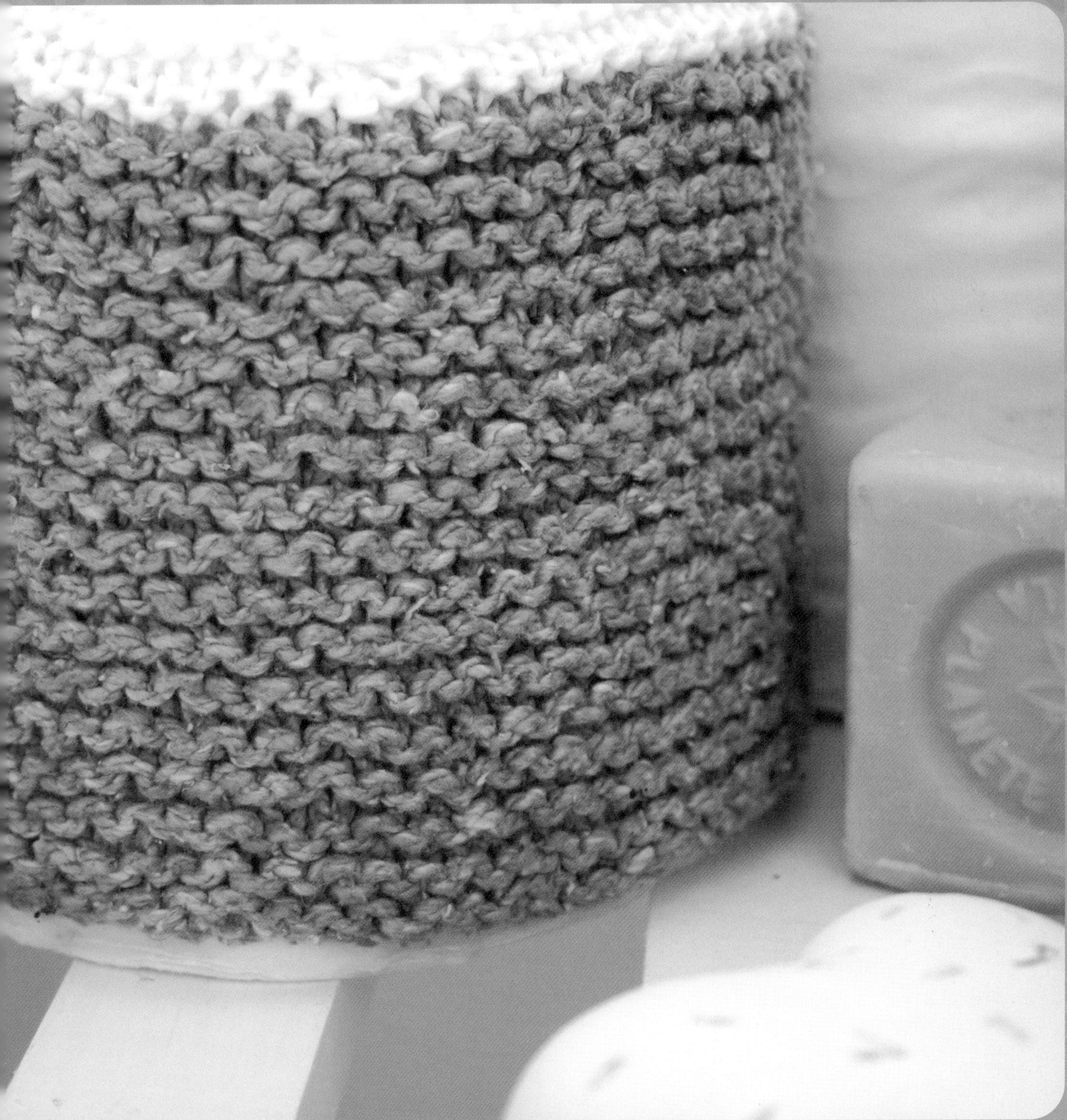

This jaunty topper starts with a basic crochet cover and gets its showtime looks from a simple brim and an added ribbon band

Terrific Topper

Materials and Equipment

- 90 yards (80 metres) of yarn
- Crochet hook
- Ribbon – ½ yard (0.5 metres)

Tension

16 trebles should produce a width of approximately 4in (10cm)

Method

Make a crochet top. If the sides are to be completed in crochet, do not break off the yarn. The example shown uses the method for crochet sides/dense cover (see also the General Instructions at the end of the book), but you can substitute a different pattern if you prefer.

Tip

Chenille or velvet-effect yarn will give this cover the effect of the soft velour that is often used to make hats

Top

Make 4ch and join into a ring with a slip stitch.

Round 1: Make 3ch (to represent the first treble); 11tr into ring. Join to the top of the 3ch with a ss.

Round 2: 3ch; 1tr in the same place as ss; 2tr into the top of each tr of first round. Join with a ss (24 trebles).

Round 3: 3ch; 1tr in the same place; (1tr in the next tr, 2tr in the foll tr) 11 times; 1tr in the next tr. Join with a ss (36 trebles).

Round 4: 3ch; 1tr in the same place; (1tr in each of the next 2tr, 2tr in the following treble) 11 times; 1tr in each of the next 2tr. Join with a ss (48 trebles).

Round 5: 3ch; 1tr in the same place; (1tr in each of the next 3tr, 2tr in the foll tr) 11 times; 1tr in each of the next 3tr. Join with a ss (60 trebles).
Fasten off.

Sides

Rejoin the yarn to the cover, or continue with the yarn used to work the top.

Round 1: Make 3ch (to represent the first treble); 1tr into the top of each treble round the edge of the top. Join with a ss.

Repeat round until the cover is long enough to reach the bottom of your toilet roll when pulled down firmly. Near the end of your work, you may feel that a further round of trebles would make it too long. In this case, work a round of double crochet instead of trebles.
Fasten off.

Note: If your yarn is finer than average you may be unable to achieve the correct tension. To make the cover wider, add extra stitches to the first round if necessary. The following technique is suitable for covers with a plain background.

To add 6 trebles, work the first round of the cover in this way: 3ch; 1tr in the same place; (1tr in each of the next 9tr, 2tr in the next tr) 5 times; 1tr in each of the next 9tr; join with a ss (66 trebles).

To add 12 trebles, work the first round of the cover in this way: 3ch; 1tr in the same place; (1tr in each of the next 4tr, 2tr in the next tr) 11 times; 1tr in each of the next 4tr; join with a ss (72 trebles).

Brim

Round 1: Make 1ch, then work 1dc into each tr. Join with a ss.

Round 2: Make 3ch (to represent the first treble); (2tr in next tr, 1tr into each of next 4tr). Repeat to end. Join with a ss.

Round 3: Make 3ch to represent the first tr; (2tr in next tr, 1tr into each of next 5tr). Repeat to end. Join with a ss. Turn work.

Round 4: 3ch; (2tr in next tr, 1tr into each of next 6tr). Repeat to end. Join with a ss. Fasten off.

Note: turning work before the final round will help it to lie flat.

Finishing

Darn in end. Neaten the ends of the ribbon and catch stitch in place.

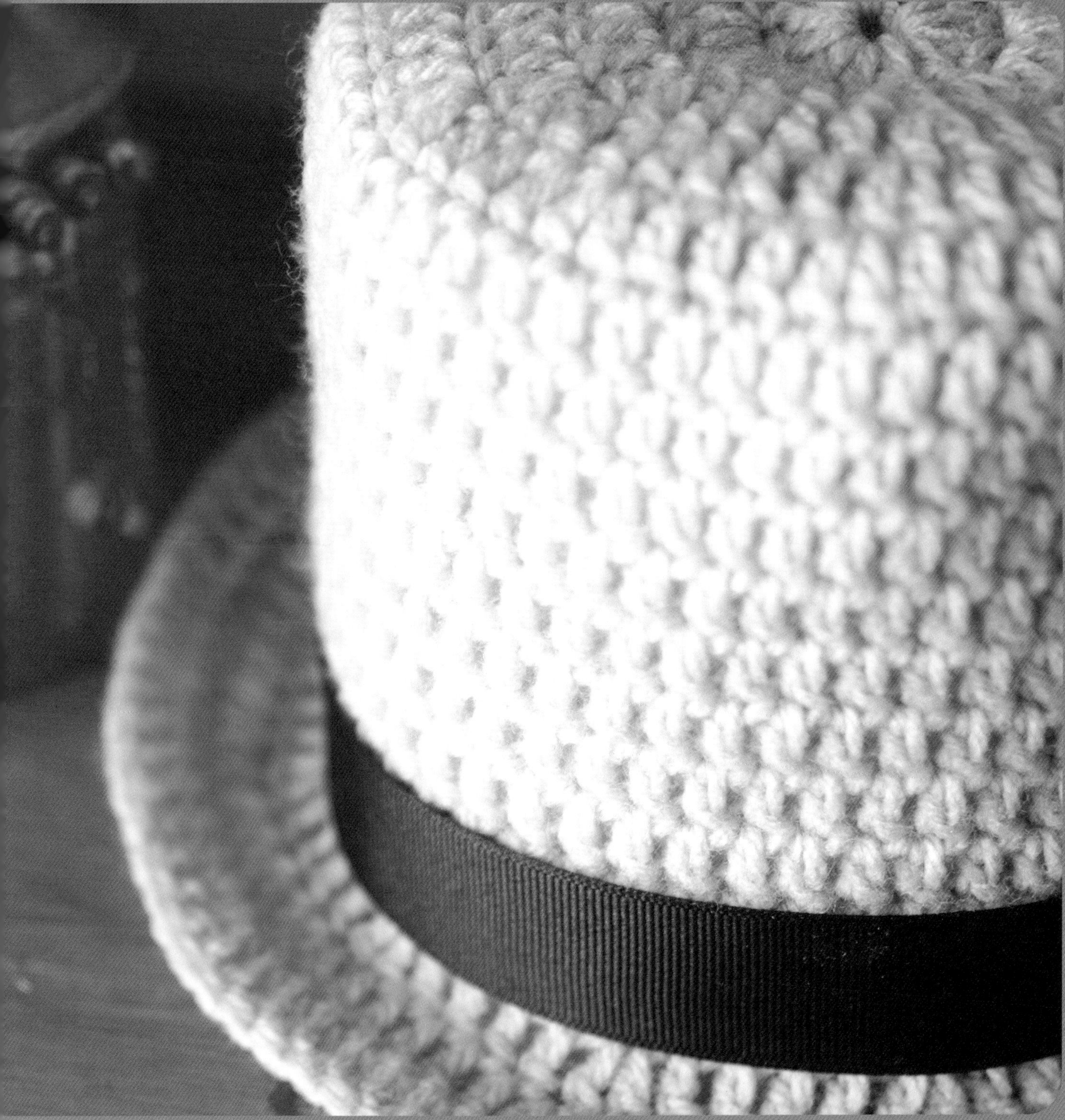

This outrageously kitsch cover makes a real impact
with just one odd ball of luxurious yarn

Fluffy Fantasy

Materials and Equipment

- 76 yards (70 metres) yarn
- Needles – straight, circular or double-pointed

Tension

21 stitches should produce a width of
approximately 4in (10cm)

Fluffy Fantasy

Method

Work in stocking stitch throughout, in the round as for the example shown, or on straight needles.

Top and sides

In the round

Cast on 80 stitches and work in the round until long enough to cover the sides of the toilet roll. Leave stitches on the needle ready to work top.

Round 1: (k2tog, k8) to end (72 stitches).

Round 2 and all even-numbered rows: k to end.

Round 3: (k2tog, k7) to end (64 stitches).

Round 5: (k2tog, k6) to end (56 stitches).

Round 7: (k2tog, k5) to end (48 stitches).

Round 9: (k2tog, k4) to end (40 stitches).

Round 11: (k2tog, k3) to end (32 stitches).

Round 13: (k2tog, k2) to end (24 stitches).

Round 15: (k2tog, k1) to end (16 stitches).

Break yarn and thread through the remaining stitches. Fasten off.

Straight needles

Cast on 81 stitches and work back and forth until long enough to cover the sides of the toilet roll. Leave stitches on needle ready to work top.

Round 1: k1; (k2tog, k8) to end (73 stitches).

Round 2 and every alternate row: p to end.

Round 3: k1; (k2tog, k7) to end (64 stitches).

Round 5: k1; (k2tog, k6) to end (56 stitches).

Round 7: k1; (k2tog, k5) to end (48 stitches).

Round 9: k1; (k2tog, k4) to end (40 stitches).

Round 11: k1; (k2tog, k3) to end (32 stitches).

Round 13: k1; (k2tog, k2) to end (24 stitches).

Round 15: k1; (k2tog, k1) to end (16 stitches).

Break yarn and thread through the remaining stitches. Fasten off.

Finishing

Join side and top seams, if necessary.

Variation

Perch a glamour doll on top of the covered roll for a modern twist on the old-fashioned 'doll in a skirt' cover.

This economical cover made from scraps of yarn is ideal for a novice knitter, as any minor errors are hidden by the texture of the work

Odds and Ends

Materials and Equipment

- 87 yards (80 metres) yarn scraps
- Straight needles

Tension

19 stitches should produce a width of approximately 4in (10cm) over garter stitch

Method

Work in garter stitch throughout. Make the top using any of the three methods shown below. The knotted yarn produces different effects according to the method chosen: the straight method creates stripes and spiral methods create rings. If you want a particularly 'knotty' appearance, push all the joins to the right side as you work.

Preparing the yarn

Tie the scraps of yarn together in a pleasing sequence. Wind them into a ball and use in the same way as regular yarn, allowing the ends of the knots to stick out of the work.

Top
Straight

Cast on 9 stitches.

Row 1: k to the last st; inc in last st.
Repeat this row until there are 23 sts on the needle.
Work 18 rows.

Next row: work to the last 2 sts, k2tog.
Repeat last row until there are 10 sts on the needle.
Cast off loosely, knitting the last two stitches together before casting them off.

Six–armed spiral from centre

Cast on 6 sts.
Row 1: inc in each st (12 stitches).

Row 2 and all even-numbered rows: k to the end.
Row 3: (inc in next st, k1) to end (18 stitches).
Row 5: (inc in next st, k2) to end (24 stitches).
Row 7: (inc in next st, k3) to end (30 stitches).
Row 9: (inc in next st, k4) to end (36 stitches).
Row 11: (inc in next st, k5) to end (42 stitches).
Row 13: (inc in next st, k6) to end (48 stitches).
Row 15: (inc in next st, k7) to end (54 stitches).
Row 17: (inc in next st, k8) to end (60 stitches).
Row 19: (inc in next st, k9) to end (66 stitches).
Row 21: (inc in next st, k10) to end (72 stitches).
Leave stitches on needle ready to complete the sides.

Eight-armed spiral from centre

Cast on 8 stitches.
Row 1: inc in each st (16 stitches).
Row 2 and all even-numbered rows: k to end.
Row 3: (inc in next st, k1) to end (24 stitches).
Row 5: (inc in next st, k2) to end (32 stitches).
Row 7: (inc in next st, k3) to end (40 stitches).
Row 9: (inc in next st, k4) to end (48 stitches).
Row 11: (inc in next st, k5) to end (56 stitches).
Row 13: (inc in next st, k6) to end (64 stitches).
Row 15: (inc in next st, k7) to end (72 stitches).
Leave stitches on needle ready to complete the sides.

Sides
Straight top

Pick up 72 stitches (9 from each side) and work until the sides are long enough to cover the roll.
Cast off.

Spiral top

Continue on the 72 sts on the needle until work is long enough to cover the toilet roll.
Cast off.

Finishing

Darn in the end of yarn that was left after casting off.

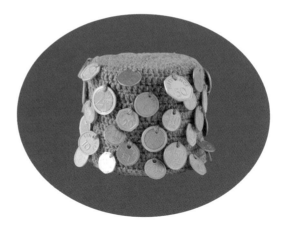

This funky cover is made using plastic money that can be bought in toy shops. The coins in the example shown are a mixture of sterling, US dollars and Euros

Cash Cache

Materials and Equipment

- 76 yards (70 metres) yarn
- Selection of plastic money
- Crochet hook
- Small drill or needle to make holes in coins

Tension

16 trebles should produce a width of approximately 4in (10cm)

Safety warning

The needle must be heated in a flame to enable it to penetrate the coins. Take great care, as molten plastic can be dangerous.

Method

Work in trebles throughout.

Top

Make 4ch and join into a ring with a ss.

Round 1: 3ch (to represent first treble); 11tr into ring. Join to the top of 3ch with a ss.

Round 2: 3ch; 1tr in the same place as ss; 2tr into the top of each tr of first round. Join using a ss (24 trebles).

Round 3: 3ch; 1tr in the same place; (1tr in the next tr, 2tr in the foll tr) 11 times; 1tr in the next tr. Join with a ss (36 trebles).

Round 4: 3ch; 1tr in the same place; (1tr in each of the next 2tr, 2tr in the foll tr) 11 times; 1tr in each of the next 2tr. Join with a ss (48 trebles).

Round 5: 3ch; 1tr in the same place; (1tr in each of the next 3tr, 2tr in the foll tr) 11 times; 1tr in each of the next 3tr. Join with a ss (60 trebles).

Fasten off, but do not break off yarn.

Sides

Continue with the same yarn.

Make 3ch; 1tr into top of each tr round edge. Join with a ss.

Continue until the cover is long enough to reach the bottom of the toilet roll when pulled down firmly. If you feel that a final round of trebles would make it too long, work the last round in double crochet instead of trebles.

Fasten off.

Note: If your yarn is finer than average it may be difficult to achieve the correct tension. For a wider cover, add extra stitches to the first round. This technique is suitable for increasing the size of all plain crochet covers.

To add 6 trebles, work the first round in this way:
3ch; 1tr in the same place; (1tr in each of the next 9tr, 2tr in the next tr) 5 times; 1tr in each of the next 9tr; join with a ss (66 trebles).

To add 12 trebles, work the first round in this way:
3ch; 1tr in the same place; (1tr in each of the next 4tr, 2tr in the next tr) 11 times; 1tr in each of the next 4tr; join with a ss (72 trebles).

Finishing

Darn in ends. Make a hole that is large enough to pass a needle through near the top of each coin, using a darning needle or fine knitting needle, heated over a flame. Alternatively, use a small drill to make the holes. They need not be very large, as they can be attached using matching thread and a fine needle rather than yarn. Attach coins randomly to the thickest parts of the cover.

Variations

- Use real coins left over from overseas trips, remembering that if you do, the finished cover will not be washable
- Decorate with small medallions or charms bought from craft suppliers
- Work the cover following the basic garter stitch pattern (see the General Instructions) and attach the coins to the ridges

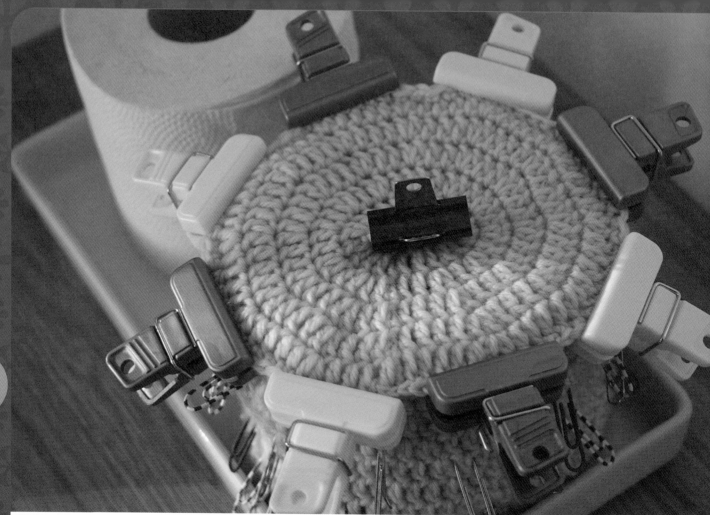

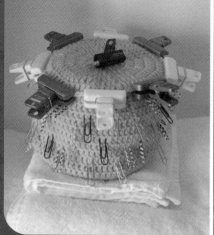

This cover makes imaginative use of everyday stationery items, and could be the perfect accessory for your office facilities

Office Supplies

Materials and Equipment

- 76 yards (70 metres) yarn
- Assorted clips in different styles and shapes
- Crochet hook

Tension

16 trebles should produce a width of approximately 4in (10cm)

Safety warning

Keep this item well away from young children as they may swallow the small parts

Method

Work a simple treble base. If your yarn is finer than average it may be difficult to achieve the correct tension. If this is the case, add extra stitches to the first round to make the cover wider – see previous project for method.

Top

Make 4ch and join into a ring with a ss.
Round 1: 3ch (to represent first treble); 11tr into ring. Join to the top of the 3ch with a ss.
Round 2: 3ch; 1tr in the same place as ss; 2tr into the top of each tr of first round. Join with a ss (24 trebles).
Round 3: 3ch; 1tr in the same place; (1tr in the next tr, 2tr in the foll tr) 11 times; 1tr in the next tr. Join with a ss (36 trebles).
Round 4: 3ch; 1tr in the same place; (1tr in each of the next 2tr, 2tr in the foll tr) 11 times; 1tr in each of the next 2tr. Join with a ss (48 trebles).

Round 5: 3ch; 1tr in the same place; (1tr in each of the next 3tr, 2tr in the foll tr) 11 times; 1tr in each of the next 3tr. Join with a ss (60 trebles).
Fasten off, but do not break off yarn.

Sides

Continue with the yarn used to work the top.

Tip

Many varieties of small clip are available from stationery stores, or use small bag clips which may be bought in supermarkets.

Round 1: 3ch; 1tr into the top of each tr round edge of top; join with a ss. Repeat until work is long enough to reach the bottom of the toilet roll when pulled down firmly. If you feel that a round of trebles would make the cover too long, finish with a final round of double crochet instead.
Fasten off.

Finishing

Darn in the ends. Add clips of your choice, attaching larger ones to the top edge and threading smaller paper clips through the material at random.

Variations

- Substitute safety pins for the paper clips
- Make a basic garter stitch cover and attach clips to the ridges of the work

The simple shape of this cover is made special by adding sparkling silver embroidered stars

Midnight Magic

Materials and Equipment

- 76 yards (70 metres) midnight blue yarn
- Small amount silver yarn (any weight)
- Straight needles
- Circular or double-pointed needles (optional)

Tension

21 stitches should produce a width of approximately 4in (10cm) over stocking stitch

Method

Work straight or in the round, in stocking stitch throughout.

Top and sides

Straight needles

Using midnight blue, cast on 17 stitches.

Round 1: (k1, inc in next st) to to last st; k1 (25 stitches).

Round 2 and every even-numbered row: p to end.

Round 3: (k2, inc in next st) last st; k1 (33 stitches).

Round 5: (k3, inc in next st) to last st; k1 (41 stitches).

Round 7: (k4, inc in next st) to last st; k1 (49 stitches).

Round 9: (k5, inc in next st) to last st; k1 (57 stitches).

Round 11: (k6, inc in next st) to last st; k1 (65 stitches).

Round 13: (k6, inc in next st) to last st; k1 (73 stitches).

Round 15: (k6, inc in next st) to last st; k1 (81 stitches).

Work straight until the cover is long enough to fit the toilet roll.

Cast off.

In the round

Using midnight blue, cast on 16 stitches.

Round 1: (k1, inc in next st) to end (24 stitches).

Round 2 and every even-numbered row: k to end.

Round 3: (k2, inc in next st) to end (32 stitches).

Round 5: (k3, inc in next st) to end (40 stitches).

Round 7: (k4, inc in next st) to end (48 stitches).

Round 9: (k5, inc in next st) to end (56 stitches).

Round 11: (k6, inc in next st) to end (64 stitches).

Round 13: (k6, inc in next st) to end (72 stitches).

Round 15: (k6, inc in next st) to end (80 stitches).

Work until the cover is long enough to fit the toilet roll.

Cast off.

Finishing

Thread a length of yarn through the centre stitches and tighten until they sit flat, with no hole. Join seam if necessary.

Embroidering the stars

Secure the silver yarn inside the cover. Make the first long stitch, then a second stitch at right angles to the first. Make two more stitches between these to complete the first star. If necessary, weave the yarn over at the centre of the stars to keep the stars flat. Repeat, working stars randomly over the sides and top of the cover as shown in the photographs.

This clever little hat would be an ideal present for a sports fan, made in the colours of his or her favourite team

Brilliant Bobble

Materials and Equipment

- 76 yards (70 metres) main yarn (M)
- Small amount of contrast yarn (C)
- Straight, circular or double-pointed needles
- Crochet hook
- Pompon maker or stiff card for templates
- Tapestry needle

Tension

20 stitches should produce a tension of approximately 4in (10cm) when slightly stretched

Method

Work in k1, p1 rib throughout, using straight needles or in the round.

Top and sides
Straight needles

Using M, cast on 73 stitches.

Row 1: (p1, k1) to last st, p1.

Row 2: (k1, p1) to last st, k1.

Repeat rows 1 and 2.

Join in C and rib 3 rows.

Change to M and work in rib until the work is long enough to reach the top of the toilet roll, with the lower edge turned back.

Next row: beg p, (rib 5, k3tog) 9 times; p1 (55 stitches).

Work 5 rows rib.

Next row: beg p, (rib 3, k3tog) 9 times; p1 (37 stitches).

Work 4 rows rib.

Next row: (p1, k3tog) 9 times, p1 (19 stitches).

Work 1 row rib.

Next row: (k2tog tbl) 9 times, k1 (10 stitches).

Thread yarn through remaining stitches and fasten off securely.

In the round

Using M, cast on 72 sts.

Work 4 rounds k1, p1 rib.

Join in C and work 3 rounds rib.

Change to M and work in rib until the cover is long enough to reach the top of the toilet roll, with the lower edge turned up.

Next round: beg p, (rib 5, k3tog) 9 times (54 stitches).

Work 5 rounds rib.

Next round: beg p, (rib 3, k3tog) 9 times (36 stitches).

Work 4 rounds rib.

Next round: (p1, k3tog) 9 times (18 stitches.)

Work 1 round rib.

Next round: (k2tog tbl) 9 times (9 stitches).

Thread yarn through remaining stitches and fasten off securely.

Finishing

Join the seam. Make a pompon and attach to cover the drawn-up stitches at the top of the hat.

Making a pompon

Cut two small circles of card approximately 1in (3cm) in diameter and cut a circular hole in the centre of each. Place the templates together. Thread a tapestry needle and use it to work in and out of the templates and round the card until the hole is full. Cut carefully through all strands of yarn at the outer edge. Prise the templates apart slightly, then tie a length of yarn securely between the rings. Leave a tail for attaching the pompon to the hat. Cut away the cardboard templates and trim any uneven ends of yarn.

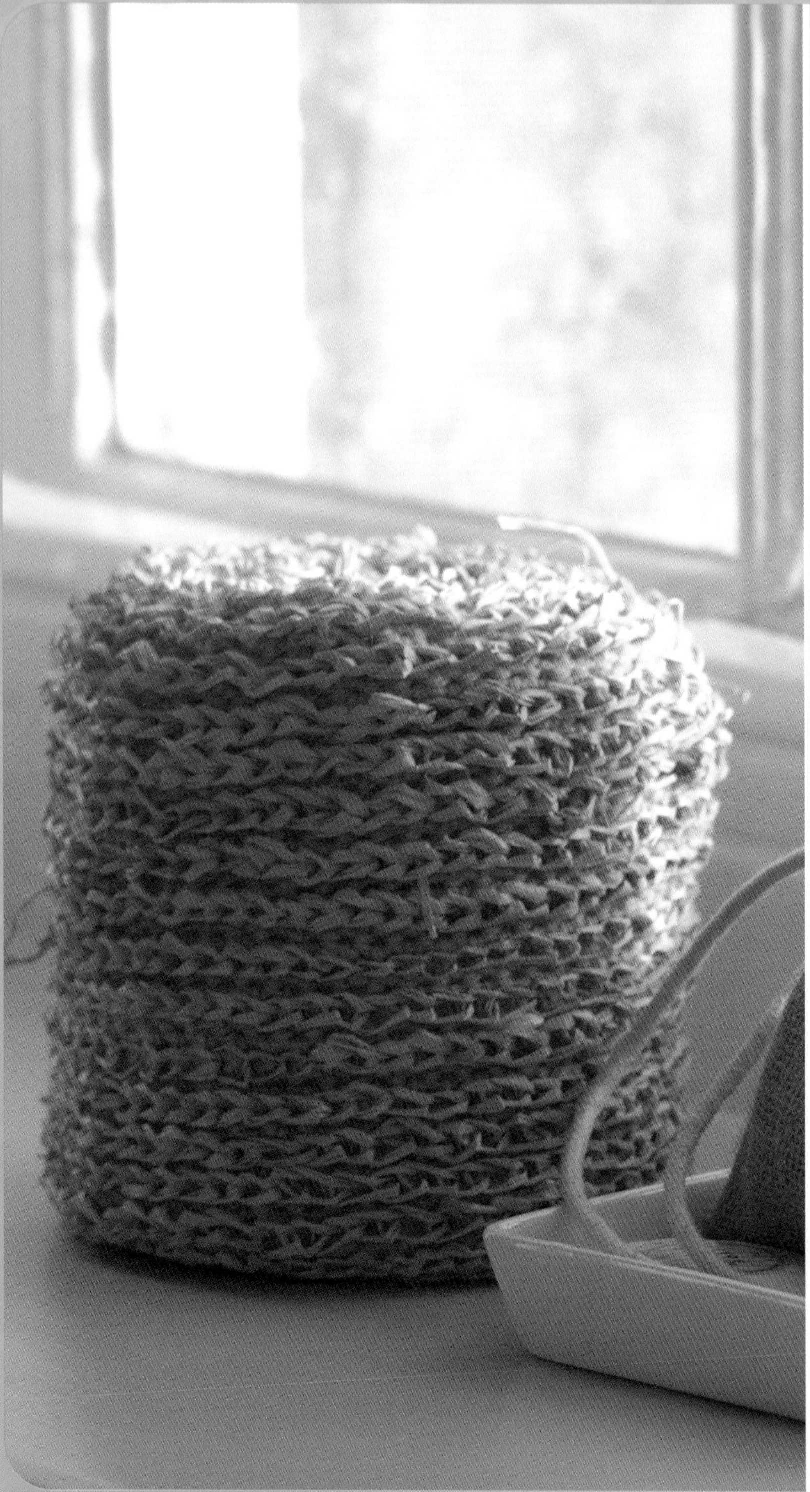

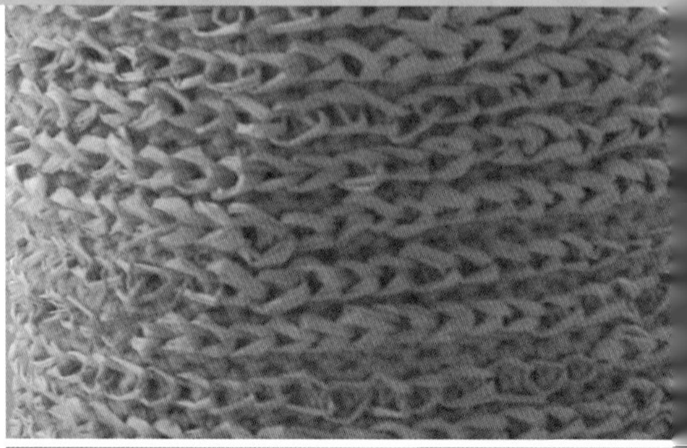

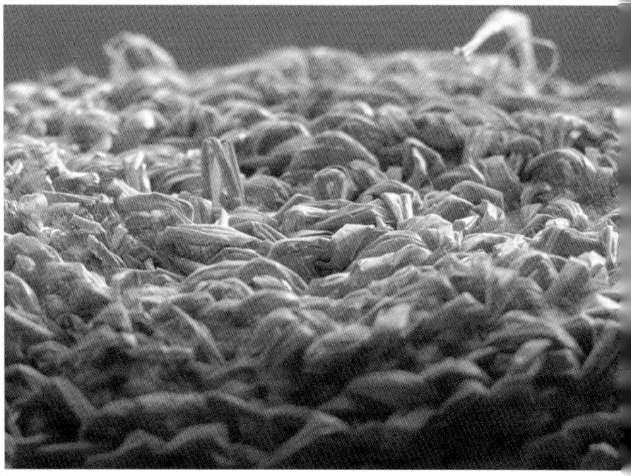

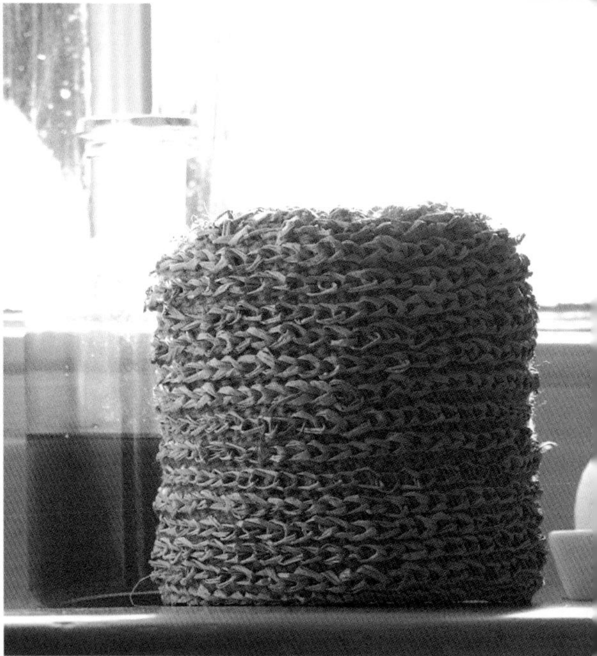

This clever cover is made to look just like a hayrick, and is ideal
for a contemporary bathroom in natural shades

Roll in the Hay

Materials and Equipment

- Raffia (available from garden centres or craft shops)
- 76 yards (70 metres) yarn, to match raffia as
  closely as possible
- Crochet hook
- Larger hook to add raffia

Tension

16 trebles should produce a width of
approximately 4in (10cm)

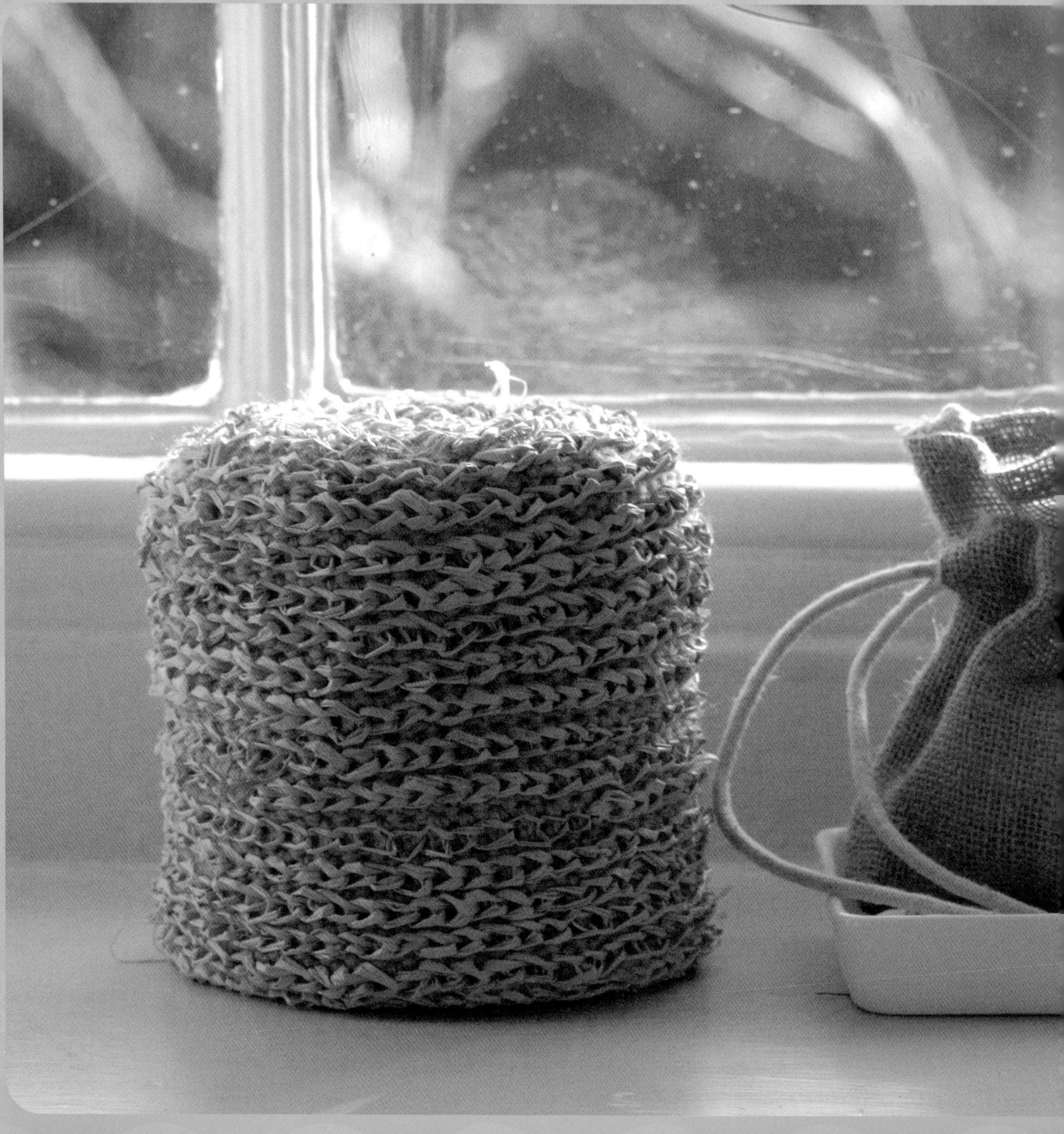

Method

Work in in a spiral, mainly in trebles with shorter stitches at the beginning and end.

Top

Make 4ch and join into a ring with a ss.

Round 1: work 4dc, 4htr and 4tr into the ring (12 stitches).

Round 2: 2tr into the top of every st from the first round((24 trebles).

Round 3: (2tr in the first tr, 1tr in the next tr) 12 times (36 trebles).

Round 4: (2tr in the first tr, 1tr in each of the next 2tr) 12 times (48 trebles).

Round 5: (2tr in the first tr, 1tr in each of the next 3tr) 12 times (60 trebles).

Note: The finished cover will not be very elastic, and the added raffia tends to fill up the inside. If your tension is tight you may need to add an extra round of trebles to the top as follows:

Round 6: (2tr in the first treble, 1tr in each of the foll 9 trebles) 6 times (66 trebles).

Tip

Raffia varies in thickness, and the finished effect should be rough and uneven: do not try to make all the stitches to the same tension

Sides

Continue on 60 or 66 trebles until work is long enough to fit over the roll. Work 4tr, 3dc and 1ss into the last 8 stitches. Fasten off and darn in the end.

Finishing

Knot the lengths of raffia together and let them fall in a heap. Do not wind the knotted raffia into a ball as it will be difficult to work with. The knots in the yarn will tend to fall on the wrong side of the work, but any that poke through will enhance the 'hay' effect.

Adding the 'hay'

Use the largest hook that will pass comfortably through the spaces between trebles. Beginning at the centre with the raffia inside the cover and the hook outside, pull a loop of raffia through the hole. Insert the hook into the next hole it will pass through. This can be quite difficult at first as the initial stitches are smaller. Pull the second loop of raffia through the first to form a chain stitch. Follow the spiral of the crochet to the end, pulling one loop through between every pair of stitches. Fasten off securely.

This cheeky chappie could make the perfect addition to the bathroom for a family with young children

Perfect Piggy

Materials and Equipment

- 87 yards (80 metres) pink yarn
- Straight needles
- Circular needle or a set of double-pointed needles
- Crochet hook
- Black felt scraps

Tension

21 stitches should produce a width of approximately 4in (10cm)

Method

Work in stocking stitch throughout. The sides may be worked straight or in the round.

Face

Cast on 10 stitches.
Row 1: inc in first st, k to last 2 sts, inc in next st, k1.
Row 2: inc in first st, p to last 2 sts, inc in next st, p1.
Row 3: as row 1.
Row 4: p to end.
Repeat the last 2 rows 4 times more (24 stitches).
Work 10 rows.
Row 23: k1, sl1, k1, psso, k to last 3 sts, k2tog, k1,
Row 24: p to end.
Repeat the last 2 rows 3 times more.
Row 31: as row 23.
Row 32: p1, p2tog, p to last 3 sts, p2tog tbl, p1.
Row 33: as row 23.
Cast off.

Sides

In the round

Using a circular needle, pick up 10 sts from each side of face (80 stitches). Work in rounds until the body is long enough to cover the toilet roll.

Straight needles

Cast on 81 stitches and work in stocking stitch until your work is long enough to cover the roll.

Snout

Sides

Cast on 30 sts. Work 3 rows.
Cast off knitwise.

Front

Cast on 4 sts.
Row 1: k to end.
Row 2: inc in first st, p to last 2 sts, inc in next st, p1.
Row 3: inc in first st, k to last 2 sts, inc in next st, k1.
Row 4: p to end.
Row 5: as row 3.
Work 5 rows.
Row 11: k1, sl1, k1, psso, k to last 3 sts, k2tog, k1.
Row 12: p to end.
Row 13: as row 11.
Row 14: p1, p2tog, p2tog tbl, p1.
Cast off.

Ears (make 2)

Side 1

Cast on 10 sts.
Work 4 rows.
Row 5: k3, sl1, k1, psso, k2tog, k3.
Row 6 and every alt row: purl.
Row 7: k2, sl1, k1, psso, k2tog, k2.
Row 9: k1, sl1, k1, psso, k2tog, k1.
Row 11: sl1, k1, psso, k2tog.
Row 12: p2 tog.
Fasten off.

Side 2

With the RS facing, pick up 1 st from each of the 10 cast-on stitches. Work rows 1–12 on these sts.
Fasten off.

Tail

Make a chain approx 2in (5cm) long and work 2 tr into each st to end. Fasten off. The tail will curl.

Finishing

Join body seam if necessary and attach face to body. Assemble the snout, stuff it lightly and attach it to the face, approximately four rows above and 10 rows below the edge.

Cut small black felt circles and attach to represent nostrils. Cut slightly larger black felt circles and attach for the eyes.

Fold ears in half along the cast-on edge and slip-stitch the outer edges together. Attach ears to the outer edge of face, at either side of the cast-on/cast-off stitches.

Attach the tail to the end of the cover, in the centre of the pig's back.

Perfect Piggy

Chains threaded through the rows of knitting give this cover
a contemporary feel that is particularly effective if you choose
a dark shade of yarn

Funky Chains

Materials and Equipment

- 76 yards (70 metres) yarn
- Straight needles
- Fine chain (see tip on page 52)
- Pliers or cutting tool to cut chain

Tension

19 stitches should produce a width of
approximately 10cm (4in) over garter stitch

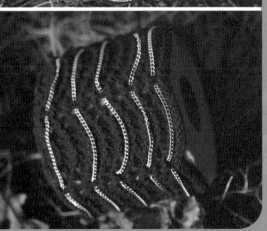

Funky Chains

Method

Work the sides in the feather and fan pattern and the top in garter stitch ridged pattern using straight needles.

Sides

Cast on 74 stitches.

Work 1 row, then work in Feather and Fan pattern:

Row 1: (right side): k to end.

Row 2: p to end.

Row 3: k1*[(k2 tog) twice, (yf, k1) 4 times, (k2 tog) twice]; rep from * to last stitch, k1.

Row 4: k to end.

Repeat these 4 rows 8 times more, or until the cover is the right length. Do not break off the yarn. Continue on the same stitches to work the top.

Top

Row 1: k1, (k2tog) twice; [k1 (yf, k1) twice, k1, (k2 tog) 4 times] 5 times, k1 (yf, k1) twice, k1, (k2 tog), k1 (62 stitches).

Row 2: k1, k2tog twice, [k2, (k2tog) 4 times] 5 times, k2, (k2tog) twice, k1 (38 stitches).

Row 3: k1, (k2tog) to last st, k1 (20 stitches).

Row 4: (k2tog) to end (10 stitches). Work 2 more rows.

Break off the yarn, leaving a long tail. Thread the end through the remaining stitches, pull tight and fasten off securely. Do not break off the yarn.

Tip

About 6ft 6in (2m) of fine chain, available from hardware or DIY stores, is enough to add five strands of decoration to the cover

Finishing

Using the rest of the tail of yarn and following the General Instructions for joining garter stitch (see page 149), join across the top and down the side. Take care to line up the curves correctly.

Applying the chain

Using pliers or a cutting tool, cut the chain into lengths to fit round your roll, allowing a little extra for the hanging curves. Thread the chain through the eyelets on either side of the 'post' on alternate rounds and sew the ends together inside the cover. Sew the joins to the roll to prevent them from slipping out of place.

Variations

- Use more strands of chain
- Vary the type of chain, perhaps using old jewellery
- Substitute the metal chains shown for crochet chains made with a bright, ribbon-type yarn

This pretty cover is smothered in flowers made in a variety of shapes
and hues – let your imagination run riot!

Coming up Roses

Materials and Equipment

- 76 yards (70 metres) green yarn
- Small balls of yarn in a variety of shades for flowers
- Crochet hook

Tension

16 trebles should produce a width of
approximately 4in (10cm)

Method

Work a plain crochet base and attach individually-worked flowers randomly.

Top

Make 4ch and join into a ring with a ss.
Round 1: 3ch (to represent first treble); 11tr into ring. Join to top of 3ch with a ss.
Round 2: 3ch; 1tr in the same place as ss; 2tr into the top of each tr of first round. Join with a ss (24 trebles).
Round 3: 3ch; 1tr in the same place; (1tr in the next tr, 2tr in the foll tr) 11 times; 1tr in the next tr. Join with a ss (36 trebles).
Round 4: 3ch; 1tr in the same place; (1tr in each of the next 2tr, 2tr in the foll tr) 11 times; 1tr in each of the next 2tr. Join with a ss (48 trebles).
Round 5: 3ch; 1tr in the same place; (1tr in each of the next 3tr, 2tr in the foll tr) 11 times; 1tr in each of the next 3tr. Join with a ss (60 trebles).
Do not fasten off. Continue with the same yarn to work the sides.

Sides

Make 3ch; 1tr into the top of each treble round edge of top. Join with a ss. Repeat until the cover reaches the bottom of the toilet roll when pulled down firmly. If you feel that a final round in trebles would make it too long, finish with a round of double crochet.
Fasten off.

Flower bases

These are made by working 10 or 12 trebles into a chain ring, then working a 'petal' over each pair of trebles. Petals should be symmetrical, with their highest point in the centre. Choose one of the examples below, or vary the stitches as desired.

Five-petal base

Make 4ch and join into a ring with a ss. Work 3ch; 9tr into ring. Join to top of 3ch with a ss (10 trebles).

Six-petal base

Make 4ch and join into a ring with a ss. Work 3ch; 11tr into ring. Join to top of 3ch with a ss (12 trebles).

Petals
Large

Work 1ss, 1dc, 1htr; 1tr into the top of the first treble of the base, then work 1tr; 1htr, 1dc, 1ss into the top of the second treble. Repeat to end. Join with a ss and fasten off, leaving a good length of yarn.

Small

Work 1ss, 1dc, 1htr into the top of the first treble of the base, then work 1htr; 1dc, 1ss into the top of the second treble. Repeat to end. Join with a ss and fasten off, leaving a good length of yarn.

Variations

- change yarn colour after the first round
- work the petals into the spaces between the trebles
- add extra stitches to each petal to create a fuller effect

Finishing

Darn in ends. Attach flowers randomly, using small catch stitches at the edge of the first row of the base, or at the edges of the petals if you want them to lie flat.

Surface crochet added to the main part of this cover stands out
to give the impression of a coiled spring

Coiled Spring

Materials and Equipment

- 55 yards (50 metres) silver-grey yarn (A)
- 33 yards (30 metres) dark grey yarn (B)
- Additional dark grey yarn for surface crochet
- Crochet hook
- Larger hook for surface crochet

Tension

16 trebles should produce a width of
approximately 4in (10cm)

Method

Work in treble, alternating the two different yarns in the sides to produce a spiral effect.

Top

Round 1: Make 3ch; 11tr into ring. Join to the top of the 3ch with a ss.

Round 2: 3ch; 1tr in the same place as ss; 2tr into the top of each tr of first round. Join with a ss (24 trebles).

Round 3: 3ch; 1tr in the same place; (1tr in the next tr, 2tr in the foll tr) 11 times; 1tr in the next tr. Join with a ss (36 trebles).

Round 4: 3ch; 1tr in the same place; (1tr in each of the next 2tr, 2tr in the following treble) 11 times; 1tr in each of the next 2tr. Join with a ss (48 trebles).

Round 5: 3ch; 1tr in the same place; (1tr in each of the next 3tr, 2tr in the foll tr) 11 times; 1tr in each of the next 3tr. Join with a ss (60 trebles).

Fasten off.

Sides

Join in B and work around the edge of the top: 1ss in each of the first 2 sts, 1dc in each of the next 4 sts, 1htr in each of the next 4 sts, then 1tr in every stitch to meet up with A. Using A, work 1 tr in every stitch to meet up with B; work trebles in B. Each stitch in A will be worked into the top of a stitch in B, and vice versa. Continue in this way until work is slightly longer than the toilet roll, as it may pull up a little when the surface crochet is added. Finish off yarns A and B on opposite sides of the cylinder, working the last 10 stitches of each as follows: 4htr; 4dc, 2ss.

Fasten off.

Tip

Surface crochet may be worked using one strand of thick yarn, or two or three strands of finer yarn. For the best effect, use metallic yarn, adding more rows for impact if necessary

Surface crochet

Work with the yarn inside the cover and the hook outside. Make a slip knot and pull to the outside through the first dark stitch at the top of the spiral. Continue along the spiral, working through the spaces between stitches rather than into the actual stitches. Pull a loop from the back through each space, then through the loop on the hook. Do not pull too tightly. Near the end of the spiral, when the spaces between the stitches become too tight to work into, fasten off.

This jolly cover is a great way to use up small amounts of yarn in cheerful primary colours

Drum Roll

Materials and Equipment

- 33 yards (30 metres) red yarn
- 22 yards (20 metres) blue yarn
- 22 yards (20 metres) white yarn
- Small amount of yellow yarn
- Straight needles
- Crochet hook

Tension

19 stitches should produce a width of approximately 4in (10cm) over garter stitch

Method

Work in garter stitch throughout.

Top

Using white, cast on 8 stitches.
Row 1: inc in each st (16 stitches).
Row 2 and all even-numbered rows: k to end.
Row 3: (inc in next st, k1) to end (24 stitches).
Row 5: (inc in next st, k2) to end (32 stitches).
Row 7: (inc in next st, k3) to end (40 stitches).
Row 9: (inc in next st, k4) to end (48 stitches).
Row 11: (inc in next st, k5) to end (56 stitches).
Row 13: (inc in next st, k6) to end (64 stitches).
Row 15: (inc in next st, k7) to end (72 stitches).
Do not cast off.

Sides

Join in red yarn and work 6 rows in garter stitch.
Join in blue yarn and work 26 rows in garter stitch.
Return to red yarn and work 8 rows in garter stitch.
Check that your work is long enough to cover the toilet roll, working additional rows in garter stitch if necessary.
Cast off.

Trim

With the RS facing, rejoin red yarn at the outer edge of the white top. Pick up and knit one stitch from each of the first row of red stitches, making sure that the white does not show through from the inside (72 stitches).
Work 4 rows in garter stitch.
Cast off.

Finishing

Join the top seam, then join the seam down the side of the cover. Join the small seam in the band on top of the drum. Using yellow, crochet a chain approximately 39in (1m) long.
Do not break off yarn as the length may require adjustment. Sew the chain in place at intervals of 12 stitches, staggering the top and bottom points of the zig-zags by 6 stitches. If you are an experienced crocheter, you may be able to attach the zig-zag points of the chain to the knitted cover as you work it.

Variations

- Use fancy yarns or add stripes
- Add a cord for carrying the drum
- Decorate the drum with fancy braid
- Add drumsticks – see method below

Drumsticks (make 2)

Using an oddment of brown yarn, cast on 24 sts and work 7 rows of garter stitch. Cast off loosely and join long edges to form a tube. Insert a pencil or the case of an old ballpoint pen, trimmed to size using a hacksaw if necessary. Close both ends of the tube. Attach the drumsticks to the top of the cover.

Note: drumsticks are not shown.

This gorgeously glitzy cover makes innovative use of the gold strip left after sequins have been stamped out, which is available from craft or haberdashery shops

All That Glitters

Materials and Equipment

- 44 yards (40 metres) gold lurex yarn (see note overleaf)
- Crochet hook
- Piece of gold sequin waste to fit round roll with a slight overlap

Tension

16 trebles should produce a width of approximately 4in (10cm)

Method

Cut a piece of sequin waste to go round the toilet roll, allowing an overlap of one hole at the join. Trim any sharp edges. Count the number of holes as one treble will be worked into each. The piece used for the example shown has 60 holes. If there are more or fewer, adjust the number of trebles worked in the final round of the top, spacing any increases or decreases as evenly as possible.

Top

Make 4ch and join into a ring with a ss.

Round 1: 3ch (to represent first treble); 11tr into ring. Join to the top of the 3ch with a ss.

Round 2: 3ch; 1tr in the same place as ss; 2tr into the top of each tr of first round. Join with a ss (24 trebles).

Round 3: 3ch; 1tr in the same place; (1tr in the next tr, 2tr in the foll tr) 11 times; 1tr in the next tr. Join with a ss (36 trebles).

Round 4: 3ch; 1tr in the same place; (1tr in each of the next 2tr, 2tr in the foll tr) 11 times; 1tr in each of the next 2tr. Join with a ss (48 trebles).

Round 5: 3ch; 1tr in the same place; (1tr in each of the next 3tr, 2tr in the foll tr) 11 times; 1tr in each of the next 3tr. Join with a ss (60 trebles).

Do not fasten off.

Sides

Continue in rounds of treble until the top extends about ½in (1cm) down the roll.

Next round: work 1tr into each hole in the top edge of the sequin waste. Work through both layers at the join.

Fasten off.

Lower edge

Work a round of trebles at the lower edge of the sequin waste (one treble into each hole). Continue in rounds until the work is deep enough to cover the toilet roll.

Note: Lurex yarns vary in weight, so you may need to work additional rounds to achieve the correct height. The work should stretch widthways to cover the roll, so the number of stitches should not need to be increased.

Variation

Following the guidelines in the General Instructions for finishing/surface crochet (see page 148), add a design to the sequin waste. The design shown has three lines of zig-zags, but count out the number of holes to make sure that it fits. The toilet roll visible through the remaining holes will create an additional effect.

This fun cover looks a bit like a shaggy wool rug, and it is made in a similar way by hooking the strands through a base of crochet

Mop Head

Materials and Equipment

- 76 yards (70 metres) off-white or cream yarn for the base
- 33 yards (30 metres) yarn for 'mop' effect
- Crochet hook to work the base
- Larger crochet hook to add fringe
- Safety pin

Tension

16 trebles should produce a width of approximately 4in (10cm)

Safety warning

If children may play with this cover, sew the final tuft of yarn in place instead of using a safety pin

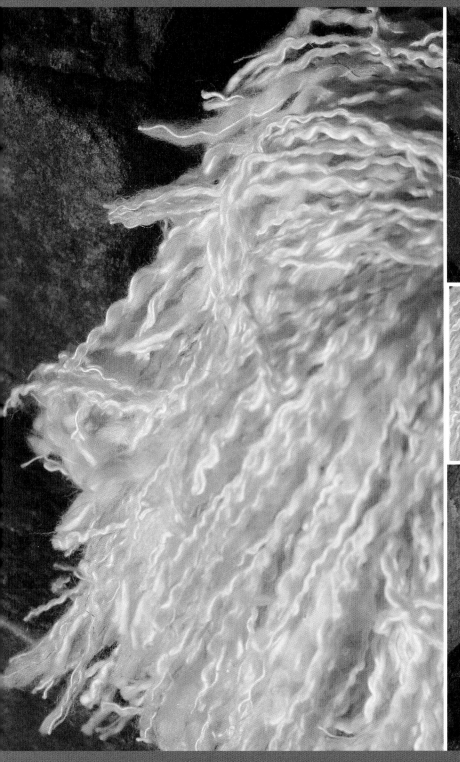

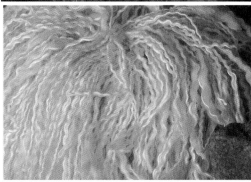

Mop Head

Tip

A textured or string-like yarn, cut into a variety of lengths, produces the best shaggy effect

Method

Follow the instructions to make a plain crochet base. To adjust the length or tighten the lower edge, finish with a round of double crochet if necessary.

Top

Make 4ch and join into a ring with a ss.

Round 1: 3ch (to represent first treble); 11tr into ring. Join to the top of the 3ch with a ss.

Round 2: 3ch; 1tr in the same place as ss; 2tr into the top of each tr of first round. Join with a ss (24 trebles).

Round 3: 3ch; 1tr in the same place; (1tr in next tr, 2tr in the foll tr) 11 times; 1tr in next tr. Join with a ss (36 trebles).

Round 4: 3ch; 1tr in the same place; (1tr in each of the next 2tr, 2tr in the foll tr) 11 times; 1tr in each of the next 2tr. Join with a ss (48 trebles).

Round 5: 3ch; 1tr in the same place; (1tr in each of the next 3tr, 2tr in the foll tr) 11 times; 1tr in each of the next 3tr. Join with a ss (60 trebles).
Do not fasten off.

Sides

Round 1: 3ch (to represent the first tr), 1tr into each tr of the previous round. Join with a ss.

Round 2: 4ch, 1dtr into each tr of previous round.
Repeat last round until the cover is the right length for your roll.

Adding the textured yarn

Cut a piece of card half the measurement you need. Wind the yarn round the card, then cut along one edge.

Cut these lengths of yarn

100 x 10in (25cm)
40 x 9in (22.5cm)
40 x 8in (20cm)
40 x 7in (17.5cm)
40 x 6in (15cm)

Finishing

Use the larger hook to knot lengths of yarn to the cover, just as if making a rug or fringe. Use two strands of yarn together. Beginning with the 6in lengths of yarn, knot into every third stitch of the third round of dtr from the lower edge. Knot the 7in lengths of yarn into the fourth round from the lower edge. Do not line them up with the previous knots, but stagger them by one stitch. Add the 8in and 9in lengths to the next two rounds of the cover in the same way. Add the 10in lengths of yarn to the remainder of the cover so that none of the background crochet is showing.

Tufted top

Fold several strands of yarn in half and pull the fold through to the inside of the loop at the top centre of the cover. Pass a safety pin through the fold and pull the tuft so that the pin fits snugly against the underside of the cover.

This zany cover is made in four identically-shaped pieces so it is easy to vary the colours – go as crazy as you like!

Jester Minute

Materials and Equipment
- 44 yards (40 metres) red yarn
- 44 yards (40 metres) yellow yarn
- Straight needles
- Crochet hook for curlicues
- 4 × small bells
- Dome for shaping top of hat

Tension
19 stitches should produce a width of approximately 4in (10cm)

Method

This design is worked in garter stitch in four sections, reversing the colours on two of the sections.

Sections 1 and 3

Using red, cast on 18 stitches and work 27 rows.

Next row: k twice into first st, k to last 2 sts, k twice into next st, k1.

Repeat the last row until there are 30 sts on the needle.

Next row: k twice into each of the first 3 sts, k to last 4 sts, k twice into each of the next 3 sts, k1.

Next row: k twice into first st, k to last 2 sts, k twice into next st, k1.

Repeat the last two rows until there are 66 sts on the needle.

Work 1 row.

Next row: cast off 24 sts, k18, cast off the remaining 24 sts.

Join yellow to the centre 18 sts and work 1 row.

Next row: work to last 2 sts, k2tog.

Repeat the last row until 2 stitches remain on the needle, k2tog.

Fasten off.

Sections 2 and 4

Make as for sections 1 and 3, but casting on with the yellow yarn and joining in the red yarn.

Tip

Cut out the dome of a disposable plastic picnic bowl to make a shaper for the inside of the hat.

Curlicues

Make a length of about 20 loose chains, or more if you prefer.

Beginning with the fourth chain from the hook, work three or more trebles into each chain. The strip will spiral round. Fasten off. Leave a tail of yarn for attaching to the hat. Work two or more curlicues in each colour.

Finishing

Join the four pieces of the hat as shown. Gather curlicues in a bunch and attach to the centre of the hat. Punch holes in the edge of the dome and sew in place inside the top of the hat. Attach a small bell to each of the points.

This clever cover made to look like the letters of a keyboard is great for computer wizards

Keyboard Skills

Materials and Equipment

- 76 yards (70 metres) main yarn (M)
- 44 yards (40 metres) contrast yarn (C)
- Straight, circular or double-pointed needles

Tension

21 stitches should produce a width of approximately 4in (10cm)

Method

Work in stocking stitch throughout. It is probably best to avoid using white yarn as the contrast yarn carried across the back may show through. White yarn also needs washing more often.

Sides

In the round

Using circular or double-pointed needles, cast on 80 stitches M and follow the chart to work the pattern.
Do not cast off; leave the stitches on the needle ready to work the top.

Straight needles

Cast on 81 stitches M.
Following the chart, work the pattern.
Do not cast off; leave the stitches on the needle ready to work the top.

Top

In the round

Continue on the 80 stitches left after working the sides in the round.
Round 1: (k2tog, k8) to end (72 stitches).
Round 2 and every even-numbered row: k to end.
Round 3: (k2tog, k7) to end (64 stitches).
Round 5: (k2tog, k6) to end (56 stitches).
Round 7: (k2tog, k5) to end (48 stitches).
Round 9: (k2tog, k4) to end (40 stitches).
Round 11: (k2tog, k3) to end (32 stitches).
Round 13: (k2tog, k2) to end (24 stitches).
Round 15: (k2tog, k1) to end (16 stitches).

Break yarn and thread through remaining stitches. Fasten off tightly.

Straight needles

Continue on the 81 stitches left on the needle after working top.
Round 1: k1; (k2tog, k8) to end (73 stitches).
Round 2 and every even-numbered row: p to end.
Round 3: (k2tog, k7) to end (65 stitches).
Round 5: (k2tog, k6) to end (57 stitches).
Round 7: (k2tog, k5) to end (49 stitches).
Round 9: (k2tog, k4) to end (41 stitches).
Round 11: (k2tog, k3) to end (33 stitches).
Round 13: (k2tog, k2) to end (25 stitches).
Round 15: (k2tog, k1) to end (17 stitches).
Break the yarn and thread through remaining stitches.
Fasten off tightly.

Finishing

Join side and top seams if necessary, matching the stitches carefully.

Keyboard Skills Chart *80 sts x 30 rows*

Each square = 1 st and 1 row. Read RS rows from R to L and WS (purl) rows from L to R.

■ **Main**
□ **Contrast**

Using the chart

The chart is worked across 80 stitches, beginning at the lower right corner. If you work the sides on straight needles, you will need to add an extra stitch to the left side of the chart. Working this in the same colour as the corresponding stitch on the right side will produce a neater join.

This striking cover is made to look just like the keys of a piano
– use ivory instead of white if you prefer

Tinkling the Ivories

Materials and Equipment
- 44 yards (40 metres) black yarn
- 22 yards (20 metres) white yarn
- Straight, circular or double-pointed needles
- Needle for embroidering keys
- Oddment of fine black yarn or embroidery thread

Tension
22 stitches should produce a width of approximately 4in (10cm) over stocking stitch

Method

Work in stocking stitch throughout. The main part of the cover is worked sideways, following the chart given for the placement of the black 'keys'. The white keys are embroidered after the knitting is completed, again using the chart as a guide.

Sides

Using white, cast on 22 stitches.
Work 4 rows.
Row 5: k12 black, k10 white.
Row 6: p10 white, p12 black.
Rows 7 and 9: as row 5.
Row 8: as row 6.
Row 10: work all stitches in white.
Continue in this way, following the chart to determine the number of rows in each block.
Fasten off.

Top edge

Turn work sideways.
Using black, pick up 81 stitches evenly from the top edge of the pattern piece. Continue in stocking stitch (if necessary) until your work is the right length to fit the roll. Do not cast off.
Leave the stitches on the needle ready to work the top.

Top

Continue on 81 stitches on needle.
Next row: (k2tog, k8) to end (73 stitches).
Row 2 and all even-numbered rows: p to end.
Row 3: (k2tog, k7) to end (64 stitches).
Row 5: (k2tog, k6) to end (56 stitches).
Row 7: (k2tog, k5) to end (48 stitches).
Row 9: (k2tog, k4) to end (40 stitches).
Row 11: (k2tog, k3) to end (32 stitches).
Row 13: (k2tog, k2) to end (24 stitches).
Row 15: (k2tog, k1) to end (16 stitches).
Break the yarn and thread through the remaining stitches. Fasten off tightly.

Finishing

Join seams. Using embroidery thread or fine black yarn and chain stitch, and following the example, embroider straight rows to define the keys.

Tinkling the Ivories

Work in stocking stitch over 22 sts and 84 rows.

Using the chart

Work up from the bottom of the chart, making the black blocks 12 stitches wide and 5 rows deep, and spacing as shown. Twist the yarns together at each colour change. The lines that define the keys are not knitted into the pattern, but are added afterwards using chain stitch (see Finishing, opposite).

 Black

White

This little fellow may be worked in any shade from off-white to dark brown – choose your favourite, or make a whole flock

Woolly Winner

Materials and Equipment

- 87 yards (80 metres) yarn for base
- 110 yards (100 metres) yarn to add 'wool'
- Crochet hook
- Larger crochet hook (approximately 6mm) to add 'wool'
- Small amount of polyester wadding
- Safety eyes or small circles of felt
- Fine black yarn or embroidery thread
- Shirring or hat elastic

Tension

16 trebles should produce a width of approximately 4in (10cm)

Method

This cover is made by hooking an extra layer of wool through the trebles of a plain spiral crochet base. Use a fancy yarn in a similar colour to the base yarn, as the base yarn will show in the face of the sheep. Do not worry about any uneven stitches as this will just enhance the 'woolly' effect.

Tip

Use a fancy yarn with slubs or curls to add the 'wool'. It may be thicker than the base yarn, but it should be a similar shade

Top

Make 4ch and join into a ring with a ss.
Round 1: 3ch; 11tr into ring. Join to top of the 3ch with a ss.
Round 2: 3ch; 1tr in same place as ss; 2tr into the top of each tr. Join with a ss (24 trebles).
Round 3: 3ch; 1tr in the same place; (1tr in the next tr, 2tr in foll tr) 11 times; 1tr in next tr. Join with a ss (36 trebles).

Round 4: 3ch; 1tr in the same place; (1tr in each of the next 2tr, 2tr in the following treble) 11 times; 1tr in each of next 2tr. Join with a ss (48 trebles).
Round 5: 3ch; 1tr in the same place; (1tr in each of next 3tr, 2tr in the foll tr) 11 times; 1tr in each of the next 3tr. Join with a ss (60 trebles).
Fasten off.

Sides

Work 1dc into each of first 4tr, 1htr into each of next 4tr. Continue in trebles until the cover is slightly longer than the roll. Finish with 4 htr, 4dc in the last 8 trebles.
Fasten off.

Adding the wool

Attach the yarn to the lower edge of the cover. With the right side facing, insert the larger hook into the next space between trebles and bring it up again in the following space. Pull the yarn through the loop on the hook to form a slip stitch round the post of the treble, make 1ch. Repeat to the top of the spiral, working a slip stitch round each post and a chain stitch between. Add wool to the outer round of the top in the same way, working the slip stitches round both trebles of the increases.
Fasten off.

Nose

Round 1: as for centre of top.
Round 2: 3ch; 1tr into the same space, 2tr into each of next 8tr, 1tr into each of next 3tr; join with a ss.
Round 3: 3ch; 1tr into the same space, (1tr in next tr, 2tr in next tr) 4 times, (2tr in next tr, 1tr in next tr) 4 times, 2tr in next tr, 1tr in each of next next 3tr.
Round 4: 3ch, 3tr, 5htr, 10dc, 5htr, 7tr. Join with a ss.
Fasten off.

Ears (make 2)

Make 7 ch. Beginning in the second chain from hook, work 5 dc into base chain.
Row 2: inc in stitches 2 and 5.
Rows 3, 5, 7, 8, 10, 12: work straight.
Row 4: inc in stitches 2 and 7.
Row 6: inc in stitches 2 and 9.
Row 9, 11, 13: dec 1 st immediately before the centre of the row and 1 st immediately after the centre.

Finishing

Using the photographs for guidance, stuff the nose and attach as shown; the dc of the final round are at the top of the nose. Embroider the features using chain stitch, and attach safety eyes or circles of felt. Work another round of 'wool' beginning and ending just before the nose. Fold the ear in half and attach to the cover, between the ridges of wool. Thread elastic through the lower edge to hold the cover in place over the roll.

This jolly addition to your bathroom looks friendly rather than fierce
– a real paper tiger!

Paper Tiger

Materials and Equipment

- 55 yards (50 metres) main yarn (M)
- 33 yards (30 metres) black yarn (C)
- Straight needles
- Circular needle (optional)
- Safety eyes
- Nose with whiskers

Tension

19 stitches should produce a width of
approximately 4in (10cm)

Paper Tiger Chart *72 sts x 24 rows*

Each square = 1 ridge of garter stitch (2 rows). Read RS rows from R to L and WS (purl) rows from L to R
The bottom of the chart represents the part nearest the face.

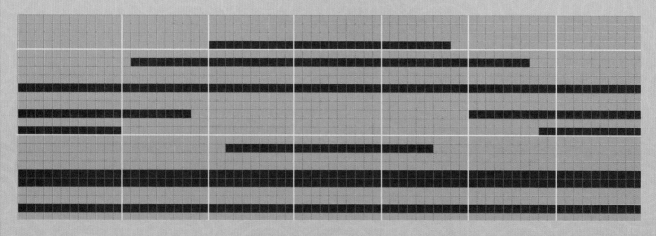

■ **Main**
■ **Contrast**

Tiger Face

The red lines show the position
for the placement of the ears.

Method

Work in garter stitch throughout. The design cannot be worked in the round as this would produce a stocking stitch finish. Always join in the black yarn on a right side row to avoid 'dotted' stripes.

Face

Using M, cast on 9 stitches.

Row 1: work to last st, work twice into last st (15 stitches).

Rep last row 5 times. Change to C.

Row 7: work to last st, work twice into the last st (19 stitches).

Rep last row 3 times. Change to M.

Row 11: work to last st, work twice into the last st (23 stitches).

Rep last row 3 times.

Work 2 rows M, 4 rows C, 6 rows M, 4 rows C, 2 rows M.

Cont in M.

Rows 33–36: work to last 2 stitches, k2tog (19 stitches).

Change to C.

Rows 37–40: work to last 2 stitches, k2tog (15 stitches).

Change to M.

Rows 41–46: work to last 2 stitches, k2tog (11 stitches).

Change to C.

Row 47: work to last 2 stitches, k2tog.

Cast off, knitting the last 2 stitches together at the same time.

Body

Straight needles

Cast on 72 stitches and work in stripe pattern until the cover is long enough to fit the sides of your roll. Work the pattern from the chart or make up your own pattern. Add more rows of garter stitch if necessary.

Cast off.

Circular needle

Pick up 72 stitches round the face on the circular needle but work back and forth as for straight needles.

Cast off.

Finishing

If the tiger is to lie down on the shelf, place the join under his chin. If he is to stand up, place it at the top of his head. Join the seam carefully from the right side, matching the stripes as accurately as possible. Attach to the face if necessary. Attach eyes and nose securely. Attach ears following red lines on diagram.

The sides of this cover are made from a series of cube-effect modules, and it looks particularly effective in subtly toning shades

Stacking Cubes

Materials and Equipment

- 55 yards (50 metres) main yarn (M)
- 17 yards (15 metres) in light contrast
- 17 yards (15 metres) in dark contrast
- Straight, circular or double-pointed needles

Tension

19 stitches should produce a tension of approximately 2in (10cm) over pattern

Method

Work in garter stitch throughout. The 'cubes' may be made individually, but it is quicker to work strips where possible.

Top

Follow the instructions below, or work the eight-armed garter stitch spiral (see the General Instructions).

Six-armed spiral from centre

Cast on 6 stitches.

Row 1: inc in each st (12 stitches).

Row 2 and all even-numbered rows: k to end.

Row 3: (inc in next st, k1) to end (18 stitches).

Row 5: (inc in next st, k2) to end (24 stitches).

Row 7: (inc in next st, k3) to end (30 stitches).

Row 9: (inc in next st, k4) to end (36 stitches).

Row 11: (inc in next st, k5) to end (42 stitches).

Row 13: (inc in next st, k6) to end (48 stitches).

Row 15: (inc in next st, k7) to end (54 stitches).

Row 17: (inc in next st, k8) to end (60 stitches).

Row 19: (inc in next st, k9) to end (66 stitches).

Row 21: (inc in next st, k10) to end (72 stitches).

Cast off loosely.

Building the strips

Using M (the lightest shade of yarn) cast on 6 stitches and work 12 rows in garter stitch (see diagram A).

Join in first contrast (the medium shade).

Row 1: k5, inc in next st.

Row 2: k4, k2tog.

Repeat the last 2 rows twice more to form a left-sloping parallelogram (see diagram B).

Change to M and work 12 rows in garter stitch (see diagram C).

Continue in this way to build up strips of squares as shown on the chart.

Cast off.

Adding sides to the squares

Turn work sideways.

Next row: Using second contrast (the darkest shade of yarn), pick up and knit 6 sts from each ridge end of the square.

Next row: k5, inc in next st.

Next row: k5, k2tog.

Rep last 2 rows once more (diagram D).

Making part-pieces

Half squares: Cast on 3 sts and work to normal height.

Other shapes: Pick up 3 sts, work slope in position shown and work straight where straight edges are shown.

Note: As some edge pieces are very small, they may be easier to work in the 'wrong' direction. It should not spoil the overall effect.

Joining

Following the chart, join the strips in the arrangement shown. Work and join in part-pieces using the chart for guidance.

Lower edging

Using M, pick up 72 stitches round the lower edge (6 from the edge of each square, 6 from each dark contrast shape and 3 from each light contrast shape). Work in garter stitch until long enough to cover the roll.

Cast off.

Finishing

Join side seam to form a cylinder and and attach the top.

Stacking Cubes Diagram

Each square = 1 ridge of garter stitch (2 rows).

 Main yarn
 Light contrast
 Dark contrast

Building the blocks

A   B   C   D

Guide for cover assembly

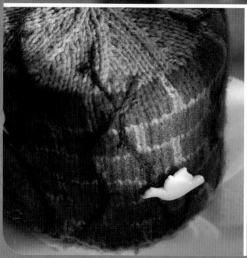

This brick-effect knitted cover is easier than it looks, and simple embroidery and a flock of tiny birds make it a real flight of fancy

Bird Sanctuary

Materials and Equipment
- 65 yards (60 metres) brick colour (M)
- 55 yards (50 metres) mortar colour (C)
- Small amount of dark green for ivy
- Straight, circular or double-pointed needles
- Decorative doves or other small birds, available from cake-decorating shops

Tension
22 stitches should produce a width of approximately 4in (10cm)

Method

Using M, work a basic stocking stitch top. Continue in pattern for the sides, noting that each perpendicular 'mortar' line on the second and subsequent rows of 'bricks' will be above the centre of one of the 'bricks' on the row below.

Top
Straight needles

Cast on 17 stitches.
Row 1: (k1, inc in next stitch) to last st; k1 (25 stitches).
Row 2 and all even-numbered rows: p to end.
Row 3: (k2, inc in next st) to last st; k1 (33 stitches).
Row 5: (k3, inc in next st) to last st; k1 (41 stitches).
Row 7: (k4, inc in next st) to last st; k1 (49 stitches).
Row 9: (k5, inc in next st) to last st; k1 (57 stitches).
Row 11: (k6, inc in next st) to last st; k1 (65 stitches).
Row 13: (k6, inc in next st) to last st; k1 (73 stitches). Leave stitches on the needle ready to work the sides.

In the round

Cast on 16 stitches.
Round 1: (k1, inc in next st) to end (24 stitches).
Round 2: k to end.
Round 3: (k2, inc in next st) to end (32 stitches).
Round 4: k to end.

Round 5: (k3, inc in next st) to end (40 stitches).
Round 6: k to end.
Round 7: (k4, inc in next st) to end (48 stitches).
Round 8: k to end.
Round 9: (k5, inc in next st) to end (56 stitches).
Round 10: k to end.
Round 11: (k6, inc in next st) to end (64 stitches).
Round 12: k to end.
Round 13: (k6, inc in next st) to end (72 stitches).
Round 14: k to end.
Round 15: (k6, inc in next st) to end (80 stitches). Leave stitches on the needle ready to work the sides.

Sides
Straight needles

Rows 1, 3, and 5: k2 M, k1 C, (k7 M, k1 C) 9 times, k6 M.
Rows 2 and 4: p6 M, (p1 C, p7 M) 9 times, p1 C, p2 M.
Row 6: k using C.
Rows 7, 9 and 11: k6 M, k1 C, (k7 M, k1 C) 9 times, k2 M.
Rows 8, 10: p2 M, (p1 C, p7 M) 9 times, p1 C, p6 M.
Row 12: k using C.
Repeat these 12 rows twice.
Continue in garter stitch until the cover is long enough to fit your roll.
Cast off.

Circular needle

Rounds 1–5: (k7 M, k1 C) 10 times.
Round 6: k using C.
Rounds 7–11: k3 M, (k1 C, k7 M) 9 times, k1 M, k4 C.
Round 12: k using C.
Repeat these 12 rounds twice more. Continue in garter stitch until the cover is long enough to fit your roll. Cast off.

Note: for either method, twist the two yarns together every two or three stitches. Vary where you do this or it may show on the outside.

Finishing

Join the side seam if necessary. Thread a length of yarn through the centre stitches of the top and tighten until they sit flat, with no hole. Fasten off securely.

Using dark green, embroider stems of ivy randomly round the sides with some spreading on to the top. Use chain stitch or stem stitch, depending on the texture and thickness of the yarn. Add small leaves at intervals. Add strands of ivy to disguise the seam and any irregularities.

Adding the birds

The birds used for the sides were on sticks and were simply pushed through the work. For the birds on top, holes were made using a heated needle. If you do this, work carefully as molten plastic can be dangerous.

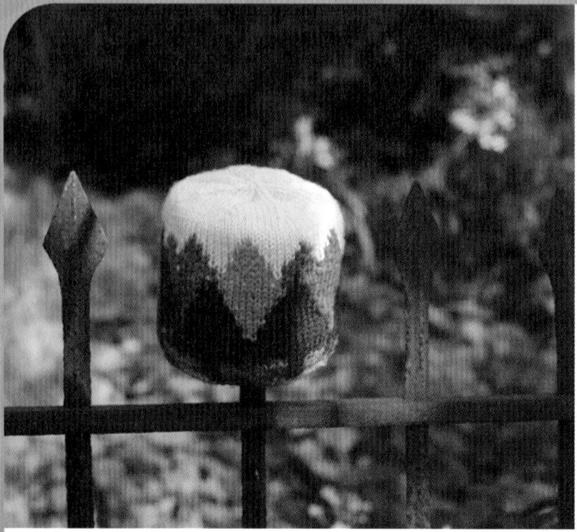

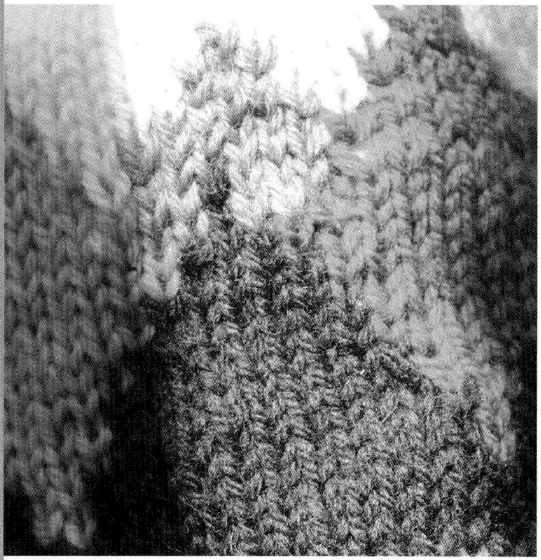

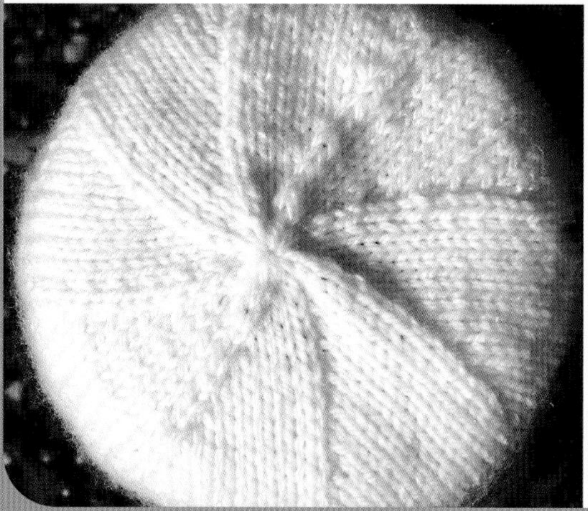

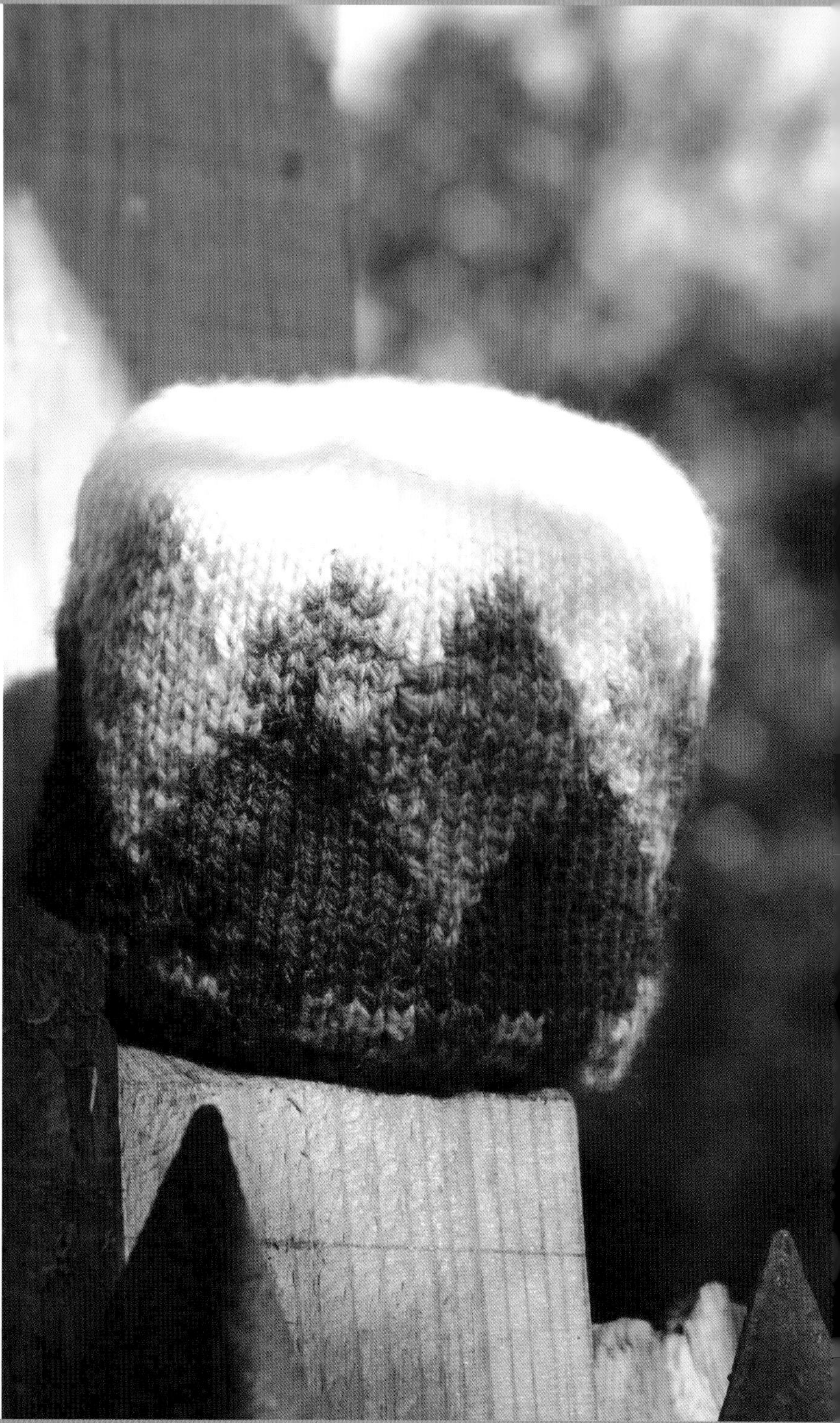

This cover is best for the more experienced knitter
because of the number of different colours used

Walk in the Woods

Materials and Equipment

- 31 yards (30 metres) blue yarn for sky
- 10 yards (10 metres) brown yarn for soil
- Small balls of yarn in various shades for tree trunks
- Small balls of yarn in various shades of green for trees

Tension

22 stitches should produce a tension of
approximately 2in (10cm)

Walk in the Woods Chart

Work in stocking stitch over 80 sts and 30 rows.

■ Earth
■ Tree trunks (1)
■ Tree trunks (2)
□ Light green (1)
■ Light green (2)
■ Medium green (1)
■ Medium green (2)
■ Dark green
□ Sky

Using the chart

It is easiest to work with short lengths of yarn and pull them through as required to prevent them from becoming tangled. Use lengths of approximately 1yd (1m) for each section and add more as required.

Method

This design may be worked in the round, but only if you are an experienced knitter. To work the design flat, follow the instructions for straight needles. For either method, use a separate length of yarn for each block and twist yarns together when you change colour.

Sides

In the round

Using soil colour, cast on 80 stitches. Work the pattern from the chart, then continue in sky blue until the cover is long enough to fit the roll.

Straight needles

Using soil colour, cast on 81 stitches and work from the chart, but add one stitch to the left side of this and every chart row. Work the extra stitch in the same colour as the first stitch of the row to make joining easier. When the chart is complete, continue in sky blue until work is long enough to cover the toilet roll.

Top

In the round

Using double-pointed needles or a circular needle, work on the 80 sts left after working the sides.

Round 1: (k2tog, k8) to end (72 sts).
Round 2 and all even-numbered rounds: k to end.
Round 3: (k2tog, k7) to end (64 sts).
Round 5: (k2tog, k6) to end (56 sts).
Round 7: (k2tog, k5) to end (48 sts).
Round 9: (k2tog, k4) to end (40 sts).
Round 11: (k2tog, k3) to end (32 sts).
Round 12: (k2tog, k2) to end (24 sts).
Round 13: k to end.
Round 15: (k2tog, k1) to end (16 sts).

Break yarn and thread through remaining stitches. Fasten off tightly.

Tip

Use darker colours for trees at the front and lighter shades for trees at the back to give a sense of perspective, and try to avoid using the same shade of yarn for two adjacent trees

On straight needles

Round 1: k1; (k2tog, k8) to end (73 sts).
Round 2 and all even-numbered rows: p to end.
Round 3: k1; (k2tog, k7) to end (64 sts).
Round 5: k1; (k2tog, k6) to end (56 sts).
Round 7: k1; (k2tog, k5) to end (48 sts).
Round 9: k1; (k2tog, k4) to end (40 stitches).
Round 11: k1; (k2tog, k3) to end (32 stitches).
Round 13: k1; (k2tog, k2) to end (24 stitches).
Round 15: k1; (k2tog, k1) to end (16 stitches).

Finishing

Darn in ends. Join side and top seam.

This cover is best for the more experienced knitter because of the pattern – but beginners can work it plain

Zig-zag Sweater

Materials and Equipment
- 55 yards (50 metres) main yarn (M)
- 55 yards (50 metres) contrast yarn (C)
- Straight needles
- Slightly smaller straight needles to work neck

Tension
22 stitches should produce a width of approximately 4in (10cm) over pattern

Method

Work in stocking stitch unless otherwise stated. If you are unsure about working the zig-zag pattern, omit it and work all stitches in the same yarn.

Body (make 2)

Using M and larger needles, cast on 37 stitches.

Row 1: (k1, p1) to last st, k1.
Row 2: (p1, k1) to last st, p1.
Repeat last two rows three times.
Change to smaller needles and repeat rows 1 and 2 three times.
Next row: (k2, inc in next st) 12 times, k1 (49 stitches).
Next row: purl to end.
Change to C. Work 2 rows.
Next row: (k2, inc in next st, k1) 12 times, k1 (61 stitches).
Next row: purl to end.
Change to M. Work 2 rows.
Next row: (k2, inc in next st, k2) 12 times, k1 (73 stitches).
Next row: purl to end.

Change to C. Work 1 row.
Next row: p to centre st, inc in centre st, p to end (74 stitches).
Next row: (k3, inc in next stitch, k2) 6 times, k1 (43 stitches).
Turn and work zig-zag pattern on these 43 sts for a total of 28 rows.

Zig-zag pattern

Row 1: (1M, 5C) to last stitch, 1M.
Row 2: (2M, 3C, 1M) to last st, 1M.
Row 3: (3M, 1C, 2M) to last st, 1M.
Row 4: all M.
Row 5: (1C, 5M) to last st, 1C.
Row 6: (2C, 3M, 1C) to last st, 1C.
Row 7: (3C, 1M, 2C) to last st, 1C.
Row 8: all C.

Note: carry yarn across all rows

Change to smaller needles.
Next row: p1, (k1, p1, k2 tog, p1, k1, p1) 6 times.
Work in k1, p1 rib for 5 rows or until cover is long enough to fit the toilet roll.
Cast off.
Complete the other side to match.
Join the open side of neck and collar.

Sleeves

Using C, pick up and knit 12 stitches from 16 rows of pattern, 1 stitch from 'shoulder', 12 stitches from 16 rows of pattern.
Work 20 rows in zig-zag pattern as for the body.
Next row: (p1, k2 tog) 8 times, p1.
Work two more rows k1, p1 rib.
Cast off.

Finishing

Join remaining seams. Catch the edge of the collar into place, if necessary. Stuff the sleeves lightly and attach loosely to the sides of the sweater.

This fun cover is styled just like a little Aran sweater – but watch out for any dolls or teddies that might steal it!

Amazing Aran

Materials and Equipment
- 110 yards (100 metres) cream yarn
- Straight needles
- Slightly smaller straight needles for inner part of neck rib

Tension
22 stitches should produce a width of approximately 4in (10cm) on main needles

Method

The Aran design is worked in rib, cable and Tree of Life panels. For clarity, instructions for each of the different panels are given separately.

Body (make 2 alike)

Cast on 37 stitches and work 5 rows k1, p1 rib.

Next row: rib 8, (inc in next st, rib 3) 6 times, rib to end (43 stitches).

Placing the panels

Work across the 43 stitches thus:
RH ribbed panel, p2 sts, RH cable panel, p3 sts, Tree of Life panel, p3 sts, LH cable panel, p2 sts, LH ribbed panel
(7+2+4+3+11+3+4+2+7= 43 stitches).

RH ribbed panel (7 stitches)

Row 1: k1, (p1, k into st below) 3 times.
Row 2: rib 7 sts.
Repeat these 2 rows.

RH cable panel (4 stitches)

Row 1: k4.
Row 2: p4.
Row 3: slip first 2 sts on cable needle and leave at front of work, k2, k2 from cable needle.
Row 4: p to end.
Repeat these 4 rows.

Tree of Life panel (11 stitches)

Row 1: k1, p4, ybk, sl1, yfwd, p4, k1.
Row 2: yfwd, sl1, ybk, k4, p1, k4, yfwd, sl1, ybk.
Row 3: FCr* p3, ybk, sl1, yfwd, p3, BCr**.
Row 4: k1, yfwd, sl1, ybk, k3, p1, k3, yfwd, sl1, ybk, k1.
Row 5: p1, FCr, p2, ybk, sl1, yfwd, p2, BCr, p1.
Row 6: k2, yfwd, sl1, ybk, k2, p1, k2, yfwd, sl1, ybk, k2.
Row 7: p2, FCr, p1, ybk, sl1, yfwd, p1, BCr, p2.

Row 8: k3, yfwd, sl1, ybk, k1, p1, k1, yfwd, sl1, ybk, k3.
Row 9: k1, p2, FCr, slip next st with yarn at back, BCr, p2, k1.
Row 10: yfwd, sl1, ybk, k4, p1, k4, yfwd, sl1, ybk.
Repeat rows 3 to 10.

*Front cross (FCr) = slip next stitch to front on cable needle, p1, k1 from cable needle)
**Back cross (BCr) = slip next stitch to back on cable needle, k1, p1 from cable needle

LH cable panel (4 stitches)

Row 1: k4 sts.
Row 2: p4 sts.
Row 3: slip first 2 sts on cable needle and leave at back of work. k2, k2 from cable needle.
Row 4: p to end.
Repeat these 4 rows.

LH ribbed panel (7 stitches)
Row 1: (k into the st below, p1) 3 times, k1.
Row 2: rib 7 sts.
Repeat these rows.

Continue working these panels until three complete branches have been worked on the Tree of Life panel. Work a further eight rows for the fourth branches but do not introduce the stitches that would begin the fifth branches.

Shape neck

(Continue to slip centre stitch as before).
Row 1 (RS): k1, p1, sl1, k2tog, psso, p1, k1, p2, cable, p1, p2tog, p2, p2tog, p1, slip1, p1, p2tog, p2, p2tog, p1, cable, p2, k1, p1, sl1, k2tog, psso, p1, k1 (35 stitches).
Row 2: rib 5, k2, p4, k6, p1, k6, p4, k2, rib 5.
Row 3: rib 5, p2, k4, p2, p2tog, p2, slip1, p2, p2tog, p2, k4, p2, rib 5 (33 stitches).
Row 4: rib 5, k2, p4, k5, p1, k5, p4, k2, rib 5.

Row 5: rib 5, p2tog, k1, p2tog, k1, p5, slip1, p5, k1, p2tog, k1, p2tog, rib 5 (29 stitches).
Row 6: rib 9, k5, p1, k5, rib 9.
Row 7: rib 9, p5, slip 1, p5, rib 9.
Row 8: rib 9, k5, p1, k5, rib 9.
Row 9: rib 9, p2tog, k1, p2tog, k1, p2tog, k1, p2tog, rib 9 (25 stitches).
Using slightly smaller needles and work 8 rows k1, p1 rib.
Change to main needles and work 8 more rows rib.
Cast off very loosely.
Make another piece exactly the same.

Shoulder join

Join neck and shoulders as far as the row where the shaping begins.
Fasten off securely.

Sleeves

With RS facing, pick up 12 stitches evenly across the 16 rows immediately below the stitching, 1 st at the join between the two halves, and 12 stitches across the first 16 rows on the second piece (25 stitches).
Row 1 (WS): k5, p4 (for cable panel), k3, slip 1, k3, p4 (for cable panel), k5.
Subsequent rows: work cable panels on the sts indicated; slip the centre st as before; p all other sts on the RS and k on the WS. Work until the fifth cable twist has been completed. Change to the slightly smaller needles.

Next row: k1, p1, k2tog, p1, k1, p2tog, k1, p3tog, k1, p3tog, k1, p2tog, k1, p1, k2tog, p1, k1 (17 stitches).
Work 3 rows rib.
Cast off tightly.

Finishing

Join remaining seams and darn in any loose ends.

This cheerful egg-head will perch happily on your bathroom shelf
– but unlike the nursery rhyme character, he is unbreakable!

Humpty Dumpty

Materials and Equipment
- 65 yards (60 metres) red yarn
- 44 yards (40 metres) fawn yarn
- Small amount of black for shoes
- Small amount of brown (B) for bricks
- Small amount of beige (M) for mortar
- Two safety eyes
- Straight needles

Tension
21 stitches should produce a width of
approximately 4in (10cm) over stocking stitch

Method

Work in stocking stitch throughout.

Wall, body and face

Using M, cast on 79 stitches.
Row 1: k2 B, (k1 M, k5 B) 12 times, k1 M, k4 B.
Row 2: p4 B, (p1 M, p5 B) 12 times, p1 M, p2 B.
Row 3: as row 1.
Row 4: as row 2.
Row 5: using M, k to end.
Row 6: p1 B, (p1 M, p5 B) 13 times.
Row 7: (k5 B, k1 M) 13 times, k1 B.
Row 8: as row 6.
Row 9: as row 7.
Row 10: using M, k to end.
Change to red and work until body reaches top of toilet roll.
* Change to fawn and work 6 rows.
Next row: (k8, k2tog) 8 times, k1 (73 stitches). Work 3 rows.
Next row: (k7, k2tog) 8 times, k1 (65 stitches). Work 3 rows.
Next row: (k6, k2tog) 8 times, k1 (57 stitches). Work 3 rows.
Next row: (k5, k2tog) 8 times, k1 (49 stitches).
Next and every alt row: p to end.
Next row: (k4, k2tog) 8 times, k1 (41 stitches).
Row 17: (k3, k2tog) 8 times, k1 (33 stitches).
Row 19: (k2, k2tog) 8 times, k1 (25 stitches).
Row 21: (k1, k2tog) 8 times, k1 (17 stitches).

Row 25: (k2tog) 8 times, k1 (9 stitches).
Row 26: p to end.
Break off yarn and thread end through remaining stitches. Fasten off securely.

Face & body separator

Working from the WS of completed piece and using fawn, pick up 79 sts along join between red and fawn. Work from * as for face but work only one row between first four shaping rows. Break off yarn and thread end through remaining stitches. Fasten off.

Arms (make 2)

Using fawn, cast on 8 stitches.
Row 1: inc in each st (16 stitches).
Work 7 rows in fawn.
Change to red and work 14 rows.
Next 2 rows: cast off 2, k to end.
Next 4 rows: dec 1st at each end.
Cast off.

Right leg

Using black, cast on 17 stitches.
Row 1: p to end.
Row 2: inc in each st (34 stitches).
Work 5 rows.
Row 8: k4, (k2tog) 9 times, k12 (25 stitches).
Row 9: p to end.
Row 10: k4, (k2tog) 5 times, k11 (20 stitches).
Row 11: p to end.

Change to red and work 14 rows.
Next 2 rows: cast off 2 sts at the beg of the row (16 stitches).
Next 5 rows: dec 1 st at both ends (6 stitches).
Next row: p2tog, p2, p2tog, casting off as you go.

Left leg

Using black, cast on 17 stitches.
Rows 1–7: work as for right leg.
Row 8: k12, (k2tog) 9 times, k4 (25 stitches).
Row 9: p to end.
Row 10: k11, (k2tog) 5 times, k4 (20 stitches).
Row 11: p to end.
Change to red and work 14 rows.
Next 2 rows: cast off 2 sts at beg of row (16 stitches).
Next 8 rows: work as for right leg.

Finishing

Attach eyes securely 12 rows above the join between red and fawn, on two of the lines of shaping. Join the back seam of the main section. Join seam in separator, leaving space to insert stuffing. Partially stuff face. Work a red V for the mouth with its centre three stitches above the join, and its outer edges two stitches above and three stitches across. Finish stuffing head. Join the remaining seam. Stuff arms and legs and attach to body. Use red yarn to attach legs to the body.

This cuddly cub is a long way from the Arctic — but he'll happily sit on your chilly china to protect your spare roll

Polar Pete

Materials and Equipment

- 220 yards (200 metres) 'fur' yarn.
- Short length of contrast yarn for casting on
- Safety eyes and nose
- Stuffing
- Needles
- Straight needles
- Circular needle or double-pointed needles (optional)

Tension

21 stitches should produce a width of approximately 4in (10cm)

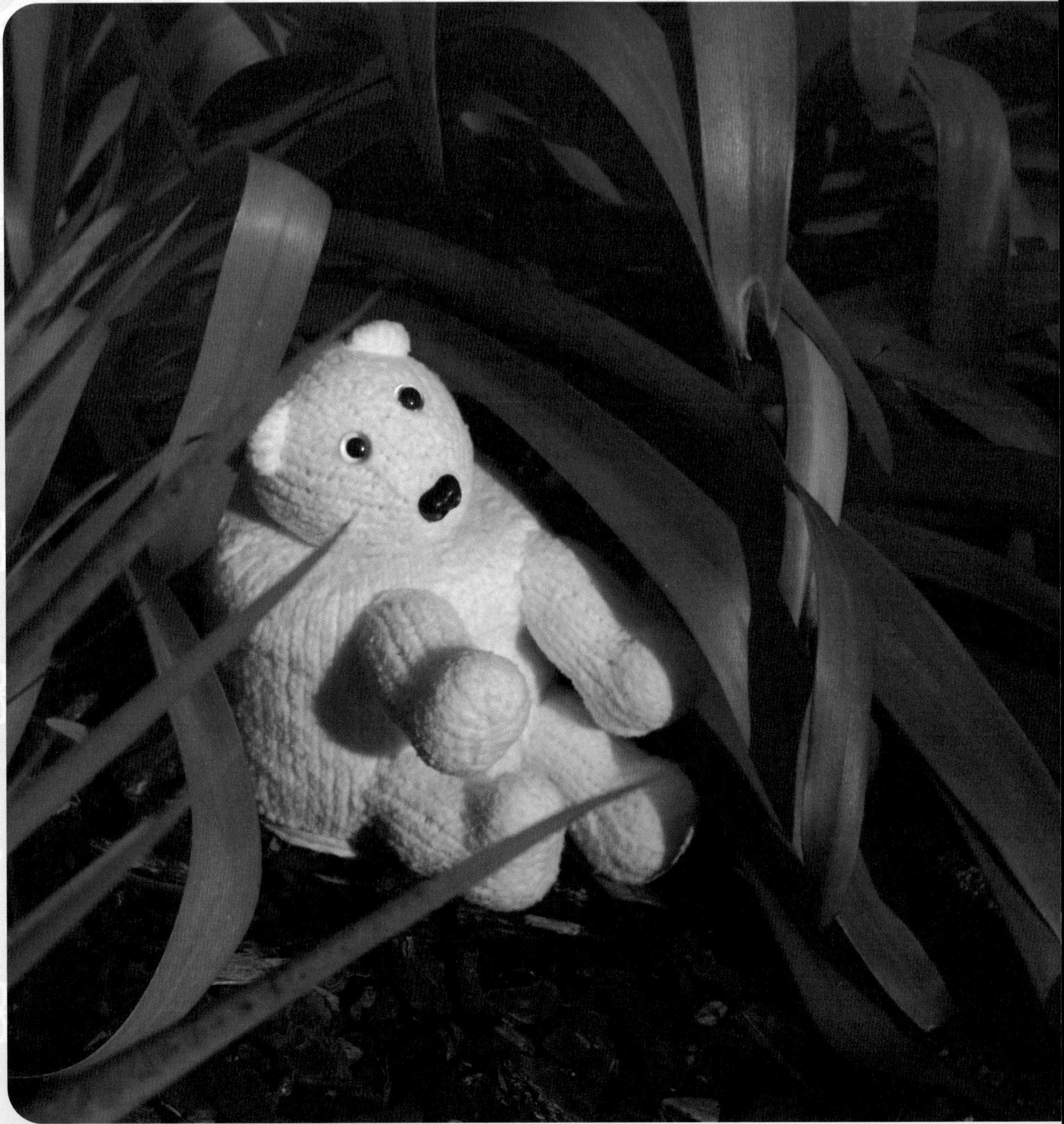

Method

Work in stocking stitch throughout.

Body

Using straight needles or working in the round, make a plain stocking stitch cover, starting at the centre (see the General Instructions).

Head

Cast on 6 sts using the length of contrast yarn (which will be removed later) and work 2 rows. Join in main yarn, leaving a 'tail' of about 8in (15cm).

Row 1 and all odd-numbered rows: p to end.

Row 2: inc in every st (12 stitches).

Row 4: (inc in next st, k1) 6 times (18 stitches).

Row 6: (k1, inc in next st, k1) 6 times (24 stitches).

Row 8: (k1, inc in next st, k2) 6 times (30 stitches).

Work 15 rows.

Nose shaping

Row 1: (k1, k2tog, k2) 6 times (24 stitches).

Row 3: k5, (k2tog, k2) 3 times, k2tog, k5 (20 stitches).

Row 5: (k1, k2tog) 3 times, k2, (k2tog, k1) 3 times (14 stitches).

Work 3 rows.

Next row: (k2tog) 7 times. Break off yarn and thread through stitches. Fasten off securely, but do not cut yarn.

Ears

Cast on 4 stitches. Work 6 rows stocking stitch.
Cast off.

Finishing head

Thread the 'tail' of yarn left at the start of the head through the first row of fur stitches. Carefully cut away the contrast yarn. Fasten off the fur yarn, but do not cut. Use the ends of yarn at each side of the head to join the seam under the head, leaving a gap to insert stuffing. Attach the nose one row above the drawn-up stitches, then stuff the head partially. Attach eyes either side of the columns of stitches in the centre of the face, approximately 10 rows above top. Finish stuffing head. Fold ears in half and join ends. Attach at the highest point of head, inner edges in line with the eyes.

Right legs (make 2)

Cast on 15 stitches.

Next row: inc in each st (30 stitches).
Work 5 rows.

Next row: k2, (k2tog) 9 times, k10 (21 stitches).

Next row: p to end.

Next row: k2, (k2tog) 5 times, k9 (16 stitches).
Work 9 rows.

Next 2 rows: cast off 2 sts at the beginning (12 stitches).

Next 4 rows: dec at both ends (4 stitches).

Left legs (make 2)

Cast on 15 stitches.

Next row: inc in each stitch (30 stitches).
Work 5 rows.

Next row: k10, (k2tog) 9 times, k2 (21 stitches).

Next row: p to end.

Next row: k9, (k2tog) 5 times, k2 (16 stitches).
Worl 9 rows.

Next 2 rows: cast off 2 sts at the beginning (12 stitches).

Next 4 rows: decrease at both ends (4 stitches).

Finishing

Fit the cover on the toilet roll. Place the head at the centre of the top and push it down so that an area about 1½in (4cm) in circumference makes contact. Attach firmly in place by stitching all round. It is a good idea to start stitching in two places, at opposite sides of the head, which will allow you to work a short way in each direction and adjust the position as necessary.

This warmly-dressed character has done his bit for wildlife conservation: his cuddly outfit is made from novelty 'fur' yarn

Chilly Charlie

Materials and Equipment

- 1 x 50g (2oz) ball of 'fur' yarn in main colour (M)
- 1 x 50g (2oz) ball of 'fur' yarn in contrast colour (C)
- Length of smooth yarn to match main
- Small quantity of yarn for face
- Straight needles
- Safety eyes
- Toy stuffing

Tension

21 stitches should produce a width of approximately 4in (10cm) over stocking stitch, but see note on page 127

Method

Work the cover and figure in stocking stitch and the contrast borders of the outfit in garter stitch.

Head

Using face colour, cast on 24 stitches.
Work 4 rows.
Next row: (k1, inc in each of next 2 sts) to end (40 stitches).
Work 21 rows.
Next row: (k2, k2tog) to end (30 stitches).
Work 1 row.
Next row: k2tog to end (15 stitches).
Break off yarn, leaving a length for joining.
Thread yarn through remaining stitches and pull tight. Fasten off.

Body

Using M, pick up and k 12 sts from the cast-on edge of head from centre front to centre back.
Join in C.
Row 1: p to end.
Row 2: k2 C, (inc in next st, k2) 3 times, inc in next st (16 stitches).
Row 3 and all odd-numbered rows: p to last 2 sts, k2 C.
Row 4: k2 C, (inc in next st, k3) 3 times, inc in next st, k to end (20 stitches).
Row 6: k2 C, (inc in next st, k4) 3 times, inc in next st, k to end (24 stitches).
Row 8: k2 C, (inc in next st, k5) 3 times, inc in next st, k to end (28 stitches).

Row 10: k2 C (inc in next st, k6) 3 times, inc in next st, k to end (32 stitches).
Row 12: k2 C (inc in next st, k7) 3 times, inc in next st, k to end (36 stitches).
Row 14: k2 C (inc in next st, k8) 3 times, inc in next st, k to end (40 stitches). Do not cast off.

Note: if your yarn is thick, fewer rows may be required to complete a half-circle that reaches to the shoulders of the figure. Omit the last few rows if the shoulders seem to be too wide.

Second half of body

Complete to the same stage, reversing all shapings.
Next row (WS): work across both sets of body stitches, keeping the contrast borders in garter stitch, until the coat reaches about half-way down the roll. Join in matching smooth yarn and work 1 row. Change to C and work in stocking stitch without borders until the cover is long enough for the roll.
Cast off.

Joining the two halves of body

Using M, pick up and knit each of the stitches along the line of smooth yarn. Work in stocking stitch with contrast garter stitch borders. On the first row, increase one stitch on each border so the borders are 3 stitches wide. At the same time, inc 10 sts evenly across row. Continue in stocking stitch with contrast borders, increasing the number of sts to produce a full effect. The number of increases necessary will depend on the weight of the yarn, but you will probably need to add about 8 stitches on each of the next three alternate rows. Knitted fur fabric conceals a multitude of sins, but space the increases as evenly as possible. Work straight until coat is almost the length required, then join in C and work 3 rows garter stitch.
Cast off.

Hood

Using M, cast on 20 sts.
Work 2 rows stocking stitch.
Row 3: k3, inc in next st (k6, inc in next st) twice, k2 (23 stitches).
Row 4 and all even-numbered rows: p to end.
Row 5: k3, inc in next st (k7, inc in next st) twice, k3 (26 stitches).
Row 7: k4, inc in next st (k8, inc in next st) twice, k3 (29 stitches).
Row 9: k4, inc in next st (k9, inc in next st) twice, k4 (32 stitches).
Row 11: k5, inc in next st (k10, inc in next st) twice, k4 (35 stitches).
Row 13: k5, inc in next st (k11, inc in next st) twice, k5 (38 stitches).
Row 14: p to end.

Shape top

Work the previous rows in reverse order, substituting k2tog for each increase thus:

Row 15: k5, k2tog, (k11, k2tog) twice, k5 (35 stitches).

Next row: p to end.

Continue in this way until 20 stitches remain.

Next row: (k2tog) to end. Thread end of yarn through sts, pull tight and fasten off securely.

Using C, pick up approx 38 sts along face edge of hood. Work one row. Cast off.

Arms

Using C, cast on 8 stitches.

Row 1: inc in each st (16 stitches).

Work 3 rows stocking stitch.

Change to M and work 8 rows.

Next 2 rows: cast off 2, work to end.

Next 4 rows: dec 1 st at each end of row (4 stitches).

Cast off.

Legs

Using C, cast on 10 stitches.

Next row: inc in each st (20 stitches).

Work 11 rows in stocking stitch.

Change to M and work 10 rows.

Cast off 4 sts on every row until all sts are worked off.

Finishing

Head

Fasten eyes to head, 12 rows above the increase row and with four stitches between each eye. Stuff head firmly. Using a length of brown yarn, embroider a shallow V-shape for the mouth, placing the centre of the V approximately four rows above the increase row. Sewing stitches can pass right through the head as they will be concealed by the hood. Turn the doll inside out and make long stitches across the neck opening to hold the stuffing in place. On the right side and with the yarn used for the face, weave a length through the row before the shaping row. Pull tight until the head takes on the correct shape. Fasten off.

Arms

Join seam and stuff firmly. Fit the cover to the roll to determine the correct position for the arms. The top edge should be level with the shoulders, and the shaped part forms the underarm. Attach from the right side.

Legs

Join seam and stuff firmly. Attach from the RS, fitting the cover to the roll to determine the correct position. Place the longest edge of the leg towards the outside of the body, and the shaped part towards the centre, with 6 sts between the legs.

Coat

Join all open seams above waist level, leaving the lower edges of the coat open. Join the hood to the first row of the coat.

Note: many novelty yarns resemble fur. Many are usually worked loosely, but must be knitted tightly for this cover. Choose yarn as close to double knitting weight as possible. Amendments may be needed to suit your chosen yarn, and in places the instructions are flexible. Adjust lengths as necessary. If the finished cover is slightly too wide for the roll it can be pulled in with elastic at the lower edge.

This proud character, complete with mortar board and 'fur' trimmed gown, could be the perfect fun gift for a new graduate

Degree of Success

Materials and Equipment

- 77 yards (70 metres) grey yarn
- 220 yards (200 metres) black 4-ply yarn
- Small amount of flesh-colour yarn
- Small amount of black yarn
- Oddment of white mohair
- Oddment of fine brown yarn
- Straight needles
- Circular or double-pointed needles (optional)
- Large needles for hair
- Crochet hook
- Stitch holder

- Safety eyes
- Stuffing
- Plastic canvas 3½in (9cm) square

Tension

21 stitches should produce a width of approximately 4in (10cm) over stocking stitch

Method

Work in stocking stitch throughout. The body section may be worked in the round if you prefer.

Head

Using flesh colour, cast on 24 sts.
Work 4 rows.
Next row: (k1, inc in next 2 sts) to end (40 stitches).
Work 21 rows.
Next row: (k2, k2tog) to end (15 stitches).
Break off yarn, leaving enough to join the back of head. Thread through remaining stitches. Pull tight.

Body

Using grey, pick up and k 24 stitches from cast-on edge of head.
Next and all even-numbered rows: p to end.
Row 3: (k2, inc in next st) to end (32 stitches).

Row 5: (k3, inc in next st) to end (40 stitches).
Row 7: (k4, inc in next st) to end (48 stitches).
Row 9: (k5, inc in next st) to end (56 stitches).
Row 11: (k6, inc in next st) to end (64 stitches).
Row 13: (k7, inc in next st) to end (72 stitches).
Row 15: (k8, inc in next st) to end (80 stitches).
Work straight until slightly longer than the height of the roll.
Cast off.

Note: if you choose to work the body in the round, read 'round' as 'row;' and work every row k.

Ears

Using face colour and straight needles, cast on 6 stitches and work 4 rows. Cast off. Fold piece in half with cast-on and

cast-off edges together. Join the short ends, then the longer seam, pulling the stitching tight so the inner edge of the ear curves inwards.

Arms

Using flesh colour, cast on 8 sts.
Row 1: inc in each st (16 stitches).
Work 7 rows.
Change to grey and work 14 rows.
Next 2 rows: cast off 2, work to end.
Next 4 rows: dec at both ends (4 stitches).
Cast off.

Right leg

Using grey, cast on 17 stitches.
Next row: p to end.
Next row: inc in each st (34 stitches).
Work 5 rows.
Next row: k4, (k2tog) 9 times, k12 (25 stitches).
Next row: p to end.
Next row: k4, (k2tog) 5 times, k11 (20 stitches).
Next row: p to end.
Change to black and work 14 rows.
Next 2 rows: cast off 2, work to end (16 stitches).
Next 5 rows: dec at both ends (6 stitches).
Next row: p2tog, p2, p2tog, casting off as you go.

Left leg

Using grey, cast on 17 stitches.

Next row: p to end.

Next row: inc in each st (34 stitches). Work 5 rows.

Next row: k12, (k2tog) 9 times, k4 (25 stitches).

Next row: p to end.

Next row: k11, (k2tog) 5 times, k4 (20 stitches).

Next row: p to end.

Change to black and work 14 rows.

Next 2 rows: cast off 2, work to end (16 stitches).

Next 5 rows: dec at both ends (6 stitches).

Next row: p2tog, p2, p2tog, casting off as you go.

Finishing the doll

Fasten eyes to head, 12 rows above increase and four stitches apart. Stuff head firmly. Using red, embroider two stitches meeting in a shallow V for the mouth. Place the centre of the V about four rows above the increase row. The sewing stitches will be concealed by the hair so they can pass through the head. Turn the doll inside out and secure the stuffing using long stitches across the neck opening. On the RS, weave a length of the head yarn through the row before the shaping row. Pull tight until the head takes on the correct shape. Fasten off securely.

Ears

Attach slightly to the front of the head. Place the lower edge about 6 rows above the increase row and curve into the correct shape.

Hair

Join seam and catch in place all round the edge.

Arms

Join seam and stuff firmly. Attach from RS, fitting cover on roll to determine correct position. The top edge of the arms should be level with the shoulders and the shaped part at the underarm.

Legs

Join seam and stuff firmly. Attach from RS, leaving approximately 6 sts between the legs. Position the longest edge of the leg towards the outside of the body, and the shaped part towards the centre.

Gown

This is made in 4-ply yarn using the same needles as for the body, to make the fabric more fluid. Increases are made on either side of marked stitches on knit rows by picking up the loop between the marked stitch and the adjacent stitch, and knitting into the back of the loop.

Cast on 33 stitches and p one row. Mark stitches 5, 13, 21 and 29 using a length of contrast yarn.

Row 1: knit, inc on either side of each marked st.

Row 2: k2, purl to last 2 sts, k2.

Rep the last 2 rows until there are 97 sts on the needle.

Next row: inc as before, and also inc before and after stitches 7, 9, 11, 43, 45, 47, 52, 54, 56, 87, 89 and 91 (129 stitches).

Work 3 rows.

Next row: k28, turn.

Next row: k2, p24, k2.

Rep the last 2 rows 10 times.

Break off yarn and place sts on a holder.

Rejoin yarn to remaining sts.

Next row: k73, turn.

Next row: k2, purl 69, k2.

Rep the last 2 rows 10 times more.

Break off yarn and place sts on a holder.

Rejoin yarn to remaining stitches.

Next row: k28, turn.

Next row: k2, p 24, k2.

Rep the last two rows 10 times more.

Break off yarn and place sts on a holder.

Rejoin yarn to first block of stitches.

Work across all sts, increasing in every 10th stitch (141 stitches).
Next row: p2, 137, p2.
Next row: k to end.
Rep the last 2 rows 5 times more. Adjust length at this stage if necessary.
Next row: k to end (this is the WS, and will form the hemline).
Work 5 more rows.
Cast off loosely.
Fold along hemline and catch hem in place using small stitches.

Hood

Cast on 13 sts and place a marker on the centre st.
Row 1: k2, p to last 2 sts, k2.
Row 2: k to end, inc 1 st each side of the marker.
Rep the last 2 rows until there are 29 sts. Continue in stocking stitch, keeping the two-stitch garter stitch border until work measures approx 2½in (8cm) from end of shaping.

Next row (RS): k10, cast off 9, k to end.
Next row: k2, p to last 2 sts, k2.
Next row: k2, k2tog, k to end.
Next row: k2, p to last 2 sts, k2.
Next row: k to end.
Rep last 4 rows until 5 sts rem.
Next row: k1, k2 tog, k2 (4 stitches).
Work 20 rows of garter stitch on these 4 stitches. Cast off.
Complete other side of hood to match.

Trim

Using white mohair, work a row of dc round outer edge of hood
OR pick up a row of stitches round the hood and cast off on the next row.

Mortar board

This is made in two separate pieces.

Cap

Using black 4-ply, cast on 25 stitches and p one row. Mark sts 4, 10, 16 and 22.
Knit rows: inc as before.
Alternate rows: p to end.
Continue until there are 73 stitches on needle. Work one row.
Cast off.

Board

Using black 4-ply, cast on 42 stitches. Work in stocking stitch until work is long enough to cover the square of plastic canvas, as follows:
Row 1: k to end.
Row 2: k1, p9, k1, p20, k1, p9, k1.

Hair

Using large needles and fine yarn to give loose 'wavy' knitting, cast on 34 stitches.
Row 1: k14, cast off 6, k to end.
Work over the first 14 stitches:
Next 5 rows: work to the last 2 stitches, k2 tog.
Cast off.
Rejoin yarn to second set of 14 sts and complete other side to match.

Finishing

Attach centre of cap to head. Attach the hair so the cap just covers its edge. Sew cap in place and attach board to cap.

A naked toilet roll!

Techniques

How to make your toilet roll decent

Measurements

An average good-quality toilet roll is about 15in (38cm) in circumference and almost 4½in (11cm) high. The cover must fit snugly but the work will stretch a little if necessary.

Yarn

All the covers shown in this book are made from standard double knitting yarn. Where decoration is added using other yarns the relevant advice is given with the pattern.

Check that you have enough yarn before starting. Crochet covers will use slightly more than knitted versions, but 77 yards (70 metres) should be enough for any of the basic covers in this book. Remember that the tension produced may vary from one yarn to another, and sometimes even from one colour to another of the same type.

Tension

Toilet roll covers are fairly small and it is easy to start again if anything goes wrong. Sometimes your work may seem to 'grow' as you proceed – so keep checking. The width must be correct, but extra rows can be added to increase the height. You may decide to go ahead without checking the tension, but if you choose to make a tension square, aim for these stitch tensions to produce a width of 4in (10cm):

Stocking stitch: 21 stitches
Stocking stitch with Fair Isle: 22 stitches
Garter stitch: 19 stitches

Crochet tension

Aim for a tension of 16 trebles to produce a width of 4in (10cm). If your yarn is finer than average and you cannot achieve the correct tension, add extra stitches to the 60 stitches of the first round.

To add 6 trebles: work 3ch; 1tr in the same place; (1tr in each of the next 9tr; 2tr in the next tr) 5 times; 1tr in each of the next 9tr; join with a ss (66 trebles).

To add 12 trebles: work 3ch; 1tr in the same place; (1tr in each of the next 4tr; 2tr in the next tr) 11 times; 1tr in each of the next 4tr; join with a ss (72 trebles).

Hooks and needles

The needles and hooks you need will depend on your natural tension. As a guide, try size 4mm or 3.75mm needles and a 3.5mm or 3.00mm hook.

Choosing your method

Some designs, such as those with patterns, can be worked only in stocking stitch. Others can only be worked in garter stitch or crochet. Many can be worked using any technique for the basic cover, or even a mixture of techniques – one for the top and another for the sides. For some designs, specific instructions are given. All instructions given use UK terminology – for US equivalents see the chart on page 155.

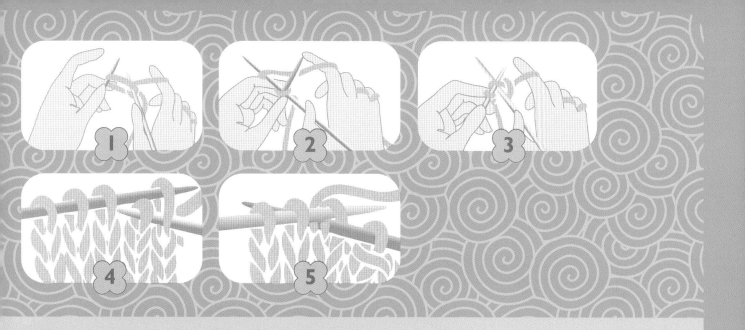

Basic techniques

The hints below should help you to solve many of the technical problems that may arise,
especially if you are not an experienced knitter or crocheter.

Casting on

1 Form a slip knot on the left-hand needle.
Insert the right-hand needle into the loop
and wrap the yarn around it as shown.

2 Pull the yarn through the first loop to create
a new one.

3 Slide it onto the left-hand needle.

There are now two stitches on the left-hand needle.
Continue until you have the desired number of stitches.

Casting off

4 Knit two stitches onto the right-hand needle, then slip the
first stitch over the second and let it drop off the needle.
One stitch now remains.

5 Knit another stitch so you have two on the right-hand
needle once again. Repeat process until only one stitch
is left on the left-hand needle. Break yarn and thread
through remaining stitch.

Knit stitch

1 Hold the needle with the cast-on stitches in your left hand. Place the tip of the empty right-hand needle into the first stitch. Wrap the yarn around as for casting on.

2 Pull the yarn through to create a new loop.

3 Slip the new stitch on to the right-hand needle.

Continue in the same way for each stitch on the left-hand needle.

To start a new row, exchange the needles so that the left needle is full once again and repeat instructions.

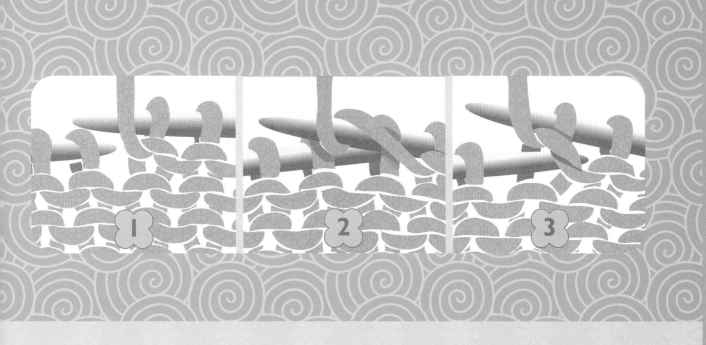

Purl stitch

1 Hold the yarn to the front of the work as shown.

2 Place the right-hand needle into the first stitch from front to back. Wrap the yarn around right-hand needle in an anti-clockwise direction.

3 Bring the needle down and back through the stitch, and pull through.

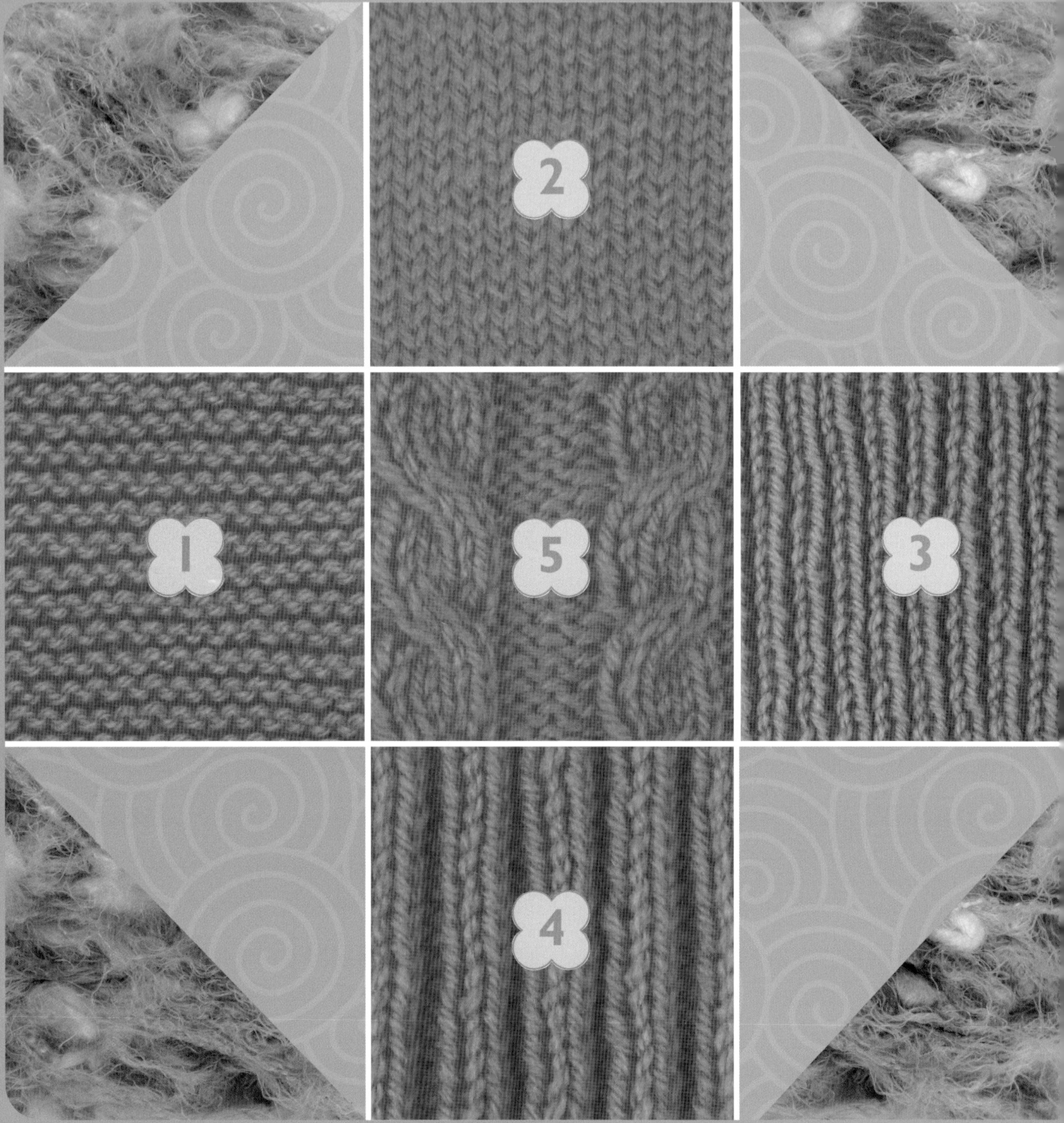
2
1
5
3
4

1 Garter stitch

Knit every row.

2 Stocking stitch

Knit on RS rows and purl on WS rows.

3 Single rib

With an even number of stitches:
Row 1: *K1, p1* rep to end.
Repeat for each row.

With an odd number of stitches:
Row 1: *K1, p1, rep from * to last st, k1.
Row 2: *P1, k1, rep from * to last st, p1.

4 Double rib

Row 1: *K2, p2, rep from * to end.
Repeat for each row.

5 Cable stitch

These decorative stitches are quite easy to produce with the help of a cable needle. Stitches are slipped on to the needle, then knitted later to create the twists.

Cable 2sts front

1 Slip the next 2 sts onto a cable needle and hold in front of work.

2 Knit the next 2 sts from the LH needle. Complete by knitting the 2 sts from the cable needle.

Cable 2sts back

3 Slip the next 2 sts on to a cable needle and hold at back of work; knit the next 2 sts from LH needle. Complete by knitting the 2 sts from the cable needle.

Working in the round

Double-pointed needles

These usually come in sets of four or five.

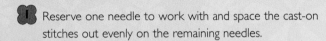 Reserve one needle to work with and space the cast-on stitches out evenly on the remaining needles.

2 When the first set of stitches has been worked, the reserved needle will take the place of the first needle and so on. Once mastered, the technique is very effective. Pull the yarn taut between each needle to avoid gaps in your work.

Circular needle

This comprises two needles joined with plastic cable, and is used to work in rounds. You may use any size of needle with any number of stitches – its length does not have to match the circumference of your work. First, mark the beginning of the round with thread, or use the cast-on tail to remind you. About a third of the way round the stitches on the needle, pull a loop of cable from between two stitches until they close to form a ring. Work until you reach the loop, then slide the next section of stitches up to the point of the needle, leaving a loop as before. As work progresses it should be possible to move more stitches at a time. Choose a slightly different place on each round to prevent stretched stitches. If you are adding patterns, it is particularly important to note where the round begins. If the loop of cable is troublesome, slip it over your wrist as you work.

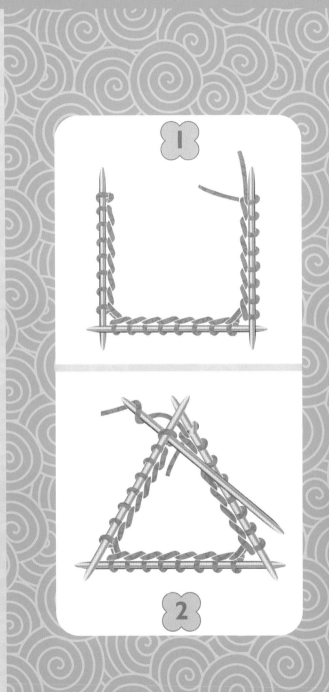

Joining seams

Joins must as invisible as possible. It is usually best to work from the right side so you can see exactly what you are getting and be sure that designs match.

Stocking stitch joins

The edges of stocking stitch tend to curl and it can be difficult to join. The best way is to use mattress stitch to pick up the bars between the columns of stitches.

 Working upwards or downwards as you prefer, secure the yarn to the top or bottom of one of the pieces you want to join. Place the edges of your work together and pick up a bar from one side, then the corresponding bar from the opposite side. Take care to stay in the same column all the way. After a few stitches pull gently on the yarn and the two sides will come together with an almost-invisible seam. Do not pull the stitches tight at the start as you will not be able to see what you are doing.

Garter stitch joins

Garter stitch lies flat and has a firm edge so is easy to join. Place the edges together, right side up, and note where the stitches line up. Pick up the bottom loops of the stitches on one side of the work and the top loops of the stitches on the other side. After a few stitches, pull gently on the yarn. The stitches should lock together and lie completely flat. The inside of the join should look the same as the outside.

Reading charts

Most charts are shown in squares, with each square representing one stitch. Charts are usually marked in sections of ten stitches which makes counting easier.

Stocking stitch

When working in stocking stitch on straight needles, read the chart from right to left on knit (RS) rows and from left to right on purl (WS) rows. Check carefully after every purl row to make sure pattern stitches are in the right position.

In the round

If you work a chart in the round, you will always be working from right to left, so you will always be able to see how the pictures or letters are forming. What you see on your work should correspond exactly with the chart.

Colour knitting

If you want to use more than one colour of yarn in a row of work, you will need to take note of some basic techniques to achieve a good result.

1 Fair Isle designs

Where two colours are used in one row do not leave long loops at the back of the work. When a colour is used over just one or two stitches, leave the other colour at the back of your work and pick it up when it is required. If either yarn needs to be taken across a space of more than three stitches, twist both the yarns together every two or three stitches.

2

The easiest way to do this is to cross one yarn from top to bottom at the first twist and from bottom to top at the next twist. This will help to stop yarns from tangling. Take care not to pull the yarns too tightly or it will gather your work in and the tension may be too tight.

3 Intarsia designs – working straight

These are designs worked using blocks of colour. Use a separate ball of yarn for each block, and twist the yarns together each time you change colour to prevent holes forming between the blocks. Remember not to pull the yarns too tightly across the back of the work.

Note: in designs where several colours are used you can combine Fair Isle and intarsia techniques by dropping some colours and carrying others.

Intarsia designs – working in the round

Beginners should not attempt to work intarsia designs in the round – they will find it easier, and safer, to work flat and join the finished piece. Experienced knitters may like to try the technique, but it can be tricky. When different blocks of colour are introduced, the work will sometimes need to be turned. This can be confusing, but it is to ensure that the yarn will be at the correct end of the block on the next round.

To work intarsia in the round, join in the yarn required for the first block and follow the first row of the chart. Odd-numbered rows will be knit rows; even-numbered rows may include purl stitches. Turn the work and work back, following the second row of the chart, and checking carefully that the stitches are placed correctly. The yarn for the block should now be in the correct position to work the third chart row. Slip the worked stitches (which belong to the second round) and return to the next section of stitches from the first round. Work according to the chart. Continue in this way until the second round is complete. Repeat the process for rounds 3 and 4.

The technique is not as difficult as it sounds, though potential problems include difficulty in following the chart and holes appearing between blocks. Take care to twist yarns together every time you change colour to prevent holes.

When one colour is to be used several times in the round, combine intarsia and Fair Isle techniques. After rounds 1 and 2 of the intarsia section you will have completed only one round with the yarn carried across the back. Complete round 2 by slipping the stitches that have already been worked, and working the others as normal.

Crochet

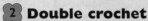 Openwork crochet

This is a useful variation on treble stitch that is produced by making 1ch between each treble stitch – see the General Instructions page 148.

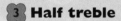 Double crochet

Start by placing hook into a stitch. Wrap new yarn round the hook and draw loop back through work towards you; there should now be two loops on the hook. Wrap yarn round hook once more, then draw through both loops; there should now be one loop left on the hook. Repeat to continue the row.

3 Half treble

Wrap yarn round hook, then place into a stitch. Wrap yarn round hook and draw the loop through; there should now be three loops on the hook. Wrap yarn round hook again and draw through the three loops. One loop should remain on the hook. Repeat to continue the row.

4 Treble

Wrap yarn round hook, then place into a stitch. Wrap yarn round hook and draw the loop through; there should now be three loops on the hook. Wrap yarn round hook and draw through two of the loops, then wrap yarn round hook again and draw through remaining two loops.

5 Chain stitch

With hook in right hand and yarn resting over middle finger of left hand, pull yarn taught. Take the hook under then over yarn. Pull the hook and yarn through the loop, holding slip knot steady. Repeat action to form a foundation row of chain stitch.

Surface crochet

Designs can be added to finished covers with surface crochet, as in the photograph below (see also page 60). The yarn used for this technique can be very different from base yarns, and you will need very little to achieve an effective result. You may need a smaller hook than usual. Hold the yarn at the back of the work and the hook at the front. Make a loop in the yarn and pull it through where the decoration is to begin. Insert the hook where you want the crochet line to continue and pull a loop of yarn through the cover and the existing loop. Make sure the first loop lies flat on the surface. Continue until the design is complete, keeping the spare end of the yarn taut and working the first few stitches over it to keep it in place. To fasten off, cut the yarn and pull the end through the final loop. Take the tail back through the cover in the same place and weave in the end using a crochet hook or tapestry needle.

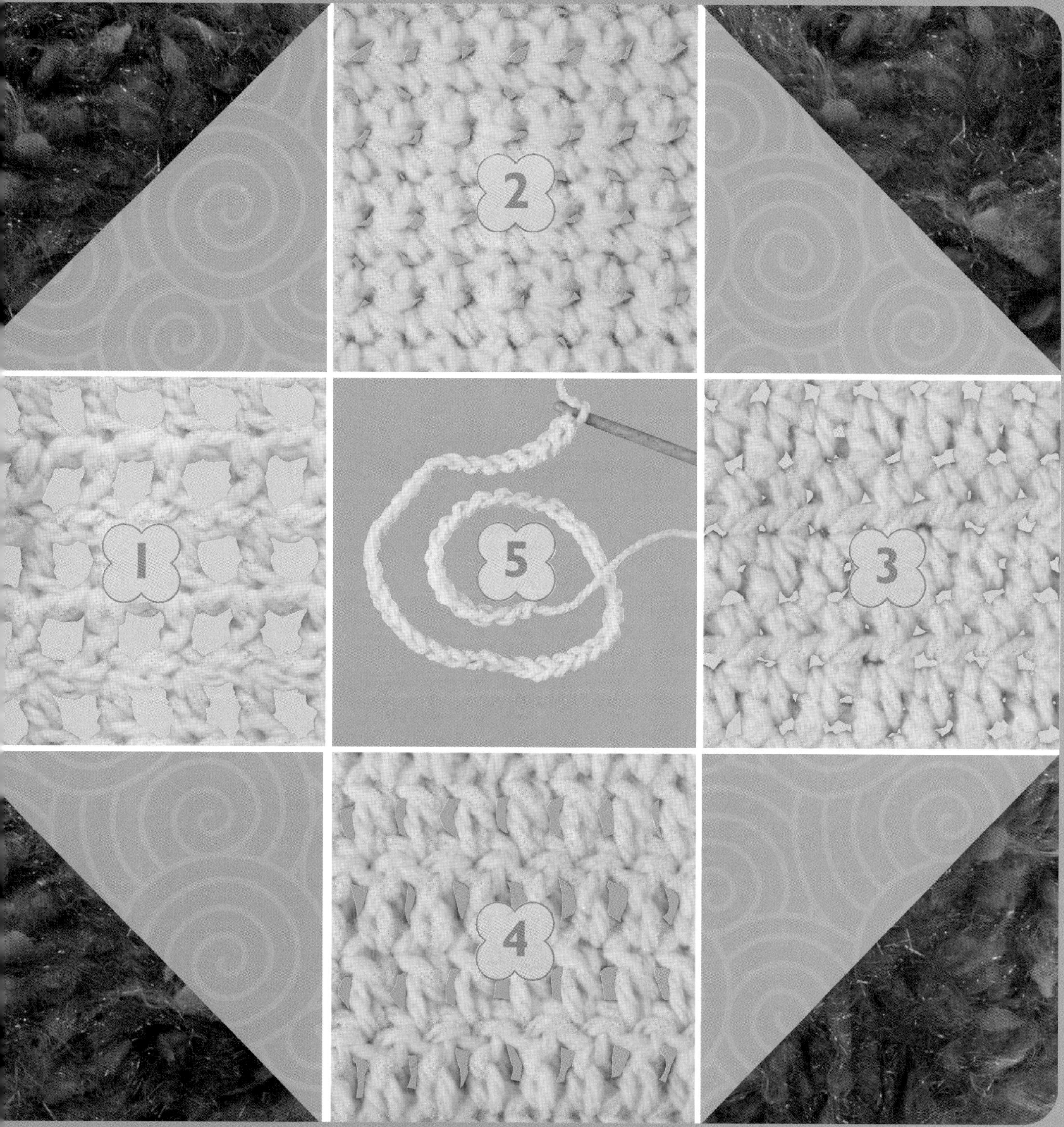
2
1
5
3
4

General instructions
Sides

Crochet sides

The sides of a basic crochet cover are usually worked over 60 stitches, to correspond to the 60 trebles in the final round of a basic top. The sides may be worked from the top, by placing the stitches in the trebles at the edge of a completed top. They may also be worked from the lower edge. In this case, the top may be made by continuing on the same stitches, or you can fasten off and join the sides to a separately-worked top. Instructions for both methods are given below.

Dense cover

This produces a plain, closely-worked fabric that is an ideal base for many different designs.

From the top

Rejoin the yarn to the cover, or continue with the yarn used to work the top.
Make 3ch to represent first tr; 1tr into the top of each tr round edge of top. Join with a ss. Continue until the cover reaches the bottom of the toilet roll when pulled down firmly. Fasten off.

Note: near the end of your work, you may find that a further round of trebles would make it too long. In this case, work a round of double crochet instead of trebles.

From the lower edge

Make 60ch and join into a ring with a ss.
Make 3ch to represent the first tr; 1tr into each ch. Join to top of the 3ch with a ss. Work in rounds until the cover is long enough to fit your roll. Fasten off, or continue to make the top.

Openwork cover

This is a more open stitch formed by working a chain between treble stitches.

From the top

Rejoin yarn, or continue on existing yarn.
Make 4ch to represent first tr and first ch; (miss 1tr; 1tr into the next tr, 1ch) to end of round. Join with a ss.
Continue until the cover reaches the bottom of your toilet roll when pulled down firmly. Fasten off.

From the lower edge

Make 60ch, plus 4ch to represent first tr and first ch; miss 5ch, 1tr into the next ch, 1ch; (miss 1ch, 1 tr into the next ch, 1ch) to end of round. Join with a ss.
Complete as for previous cover.

Knitted sides

You may work knitted sides in garter stitch or stocking stitch. Garter stitch sides must be worked back and forth on straight needles or a circular needle. Stocking stitch tops may be worked on straight needles or in the round. You may find it easier to work the sides and top separately then join them.

Garter stitch sides

Cast on 72 sts, or pick up and knit 72 sts round the edges of a previously-completed top. Work in garter stitch (every row knit) until the sides are the correct height. Cast off.

Stocking stitch sides

There are several different methods of working stocking stitch sides, so choose the one that suits you from the four that follow. Working in the round is the same whether you work on a set of double-pointed needles or a circular needle.

Straight needles – from the top

Pick up 81 sts or continue on existing sts, noting that this will only be possible if the top you are picking up from is not yet joined into a complete circle. Work back and forth, 1 row k, 1 row p, until the sides are the correct height. Cast off.

Straight needles – from the lower edge

Cast on 81 sts and work in stocking stitch until the sides are the correct height. Cast off, or continue on the same sts to complete a top worked from the outside.

In the round – from the top

Using a circular needle or double-pointed needles, pick up 80 sts or continue on existing sts. Knit every round until the sides are the correct height. Cast off.

In the round – from the lower edge

Using a circular needle or double-pointed needles, cast on 80 sts and join into a ring. Work until the sides are the correct height for the roll. Cast off or leave the stitches on the needle ready to make the top.

Note: it can be difficult to join the first row without twisting the work. One solution is to work a few rows of stocking stitch (as if working on straight needles), then change to working in rounds and join the small seam at the bottom afterwards.

Variations

Try making a distinct line between the top and the sides. To do this when using straight needles, work one row knit on the wrong (purl) side. To do this in the round, work one row purl.

General instructions
Tops

Crochet top

This basic top may be used with any of the crochet patterns in this book.

Method
Make 4ch and join into a ring with a ss.
Round 1: 3ch (to represent first tr); 11tr into ring. Join to top of 3ch with a ss.
Round 2: 3ch; 1tr in the same place as ss; 2tr into the top of each tr of first round. Join using a ss (24 trebles).
Round 3: 3ch; 1tr in the same place; (1tr in the next tr, 2tr in the foll tr) 11 times; 1tr in the next tr. Join with a ss (36 trebles).
Round 4: 3ch; 1tr in the same place; (1tr in each of the next 2tr, 2tr in the foll tr) 11 times; 1tr in each of the next 2tr. Join with a ss (48 trebles).
Round 5: 3ch; 1tr in the same place; (1tr in each of the next 3tr, 2tr in the foll tr) 11 times; 1tr in each of the next 3tr. Join with a ss (60 trebles).
Fasten off. If a change of colour or technique is needed, break off yarn.

Note: do not fasten off if the sides are to be completed in crochet.

Garter stitch tops

These are worked back and forth, every row knit. For most designs the straight and spiral tops are interchangeable; the side of the cover may determine your choice. Increase is by knitting twice into a stitch or in any way that you prefer.

Straight
This produces an octagonal shape, with each side equivalent to 9 sts in width. It pulls into a round when the sides are attached.

Method

Cast on 9 sts.

Row 1: k to the last st; inc in last st.

Rep this row until there are 23 sts on the needle.

Work 18 rows straight.

Next row: work to the last 2 sts; k2tog.

Rep this row until there are 10 sts on the needle.

Cast off loosely, knitting the last two sts together before casting them off.

Six-armed spiral from centre

This is worked from the centre and has a circular edge.

Method

Cast on 6 sts.

Row 1: inc in each st (12 sts).

Row 2 and all even-numbered rows: k to end.

Row 3: (inc in next st, k1) to end (18 sts).

Row 5: (inc in next st, k2) to end (24 sts).

Row 7: (inc in next st, k3) to end (30 sts).

Row 9: (inc in next st, k4) to end (36 sts).

Row 11: (inc in next st, k5) to end (42 sts).

Row 13: (inc in next st, k6) to end (48 sts).

Row 15: (inc in next st, k7) to end (54 sts).

Row 17: (inc in next st, k8) to end (60 sts).

Row 19: (inc in next st, k9) to end (66 sts).

Row 21: (inc in next st, k10) to end (72 sts).

Cast off loosely if required, or leave sts on needle ready to complete sides of cover.

Eight-armed spiral from centre

This has a circular shape in eight sections. Sides can be worked on the stitches left on the needle after it is completed.

Method

Cast on 8 sts.

Row 1: inc in each st (16 stitches).

Row 2 and all even-numbered rows: k to end.

Row 3: (inc in next st, k1) to end (24 stitches).

Row 5: (inc in next st, k2) to end (32 stitches).

Row 7: (inc in next st, k3) to end (40 stitches).

Row 9: (inc in next st, k4) to end (48 stitches).

Row 11: (inc in next st, k5) to end (56 stitches).

Row 13: (inc in next st, k6) to end (64 stitches).

Row 15: (inc in next st, k7) to end (72 stitches).

Techniques

Six-armed spiral inwards

This is worked from the outside in. If you have worked the sides first, simply leave the stitches on the needle and continue.

Method

Pick up and knit 72 sts, then work 1 row OR continue on 72 sts left on needle after working sides and work 2 rows.

Row 1: (k2tog, k10) to end of row (66 stitches).

Row 2 and all even-numbered rows to row 18: k to end.

Row 5: (k2tog, k9) to end of row (60 stitches).

Row 7: (k2tog, k8) to end of row (54 stitches).

Row 9: (k2tog, k7) to end of row (48 stitches).

Row 11: (k2tog, k6) to end of row (42 stitches).

Row 13: (k2tog, k5) to end of row (36 stitches).

Row 15: (k2tog, k3) to end of row (24 stitches).

Row 17: (k2tog, k2) to end of row (18 stitches).

Row 19: (k2tog, k1) to end of row (12 stitches).

Row 20: (k2tog) to end of row (6 stitches).

Break off yarn. Thread end through remaining stitches and fasten off securely.

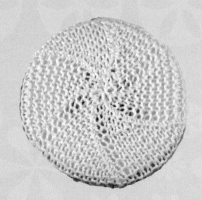

Eight-armed spiral inwards (not shown)

This can also be worked on stitches left on the needle after working the sides. It tends to produce a smaller top, which is useful if your natural tension is loose.

Method

Pick up and knit 72 stitches, then work 1 row OR continue on stitches left on needle after working sides and work 2 rows.

Row 3: (k2tog, k7) to the end of the row (64 stitches).

Row 2 and all even-numbered rows: k to end.

Row 5: (k2tog, k6) to end of row (56 stitches).

Row 7: (k2tog, k5) to end of row (48 stitches).

Row 9: (k2tog, k4) to end of row (40 stitches).

Row 11: (k2tog, k3) to end of row (32 stitches).

Row 13: (k2tog, k2) to end of row (24 stitches).

Row 15: (k2tog, k1) to end of row (16 stitches).

Row 17: (k2tog) to end of row (8 stitches).

Break off yarn. Thread end through remaining stitches and fasten off securely.

Stocking stitch tops

These tops can be made on straight needles or in the round. Different methods of increasing or decreasing may be used but may produce more, or less, obvious spirals. The spacing between the increases or decreases must remain the same.

In the round

If you choose to make a top that begins at the centre, the stitches can be left on the needle after it is completed, ready to work the sides. If you choose to work a top that begins at the edge, you may wish to make the sides first and continue on the same stitches for the top.

Starting from the centre

Cast on 16 stitches.

Round 1: (k1, inc in next st) to end (24 stitches).
Round 2 and all even-numbered rounds: k to end.
Round 3: (k2, inc in next st) to end (32 stitches).
Round 5: (k3, inc in next st) to end (40 stitches).
Round 7: (k4, inc in next st) to end (48 stitches).
Round 9: (k5, inc in next st) to end (56 stitches).
Round 11: (k6, inc in next st) to end (64 stitches).
Round 13: (k6, inc in next st) to end (72 stitches).
Round 15: (k6, inc in next st) to end (80 stitches).

Cast off, or leave stitches on needle ready to work sides. Thread a length of yarn through centre stitches and tighten until they sit flat, with no hole. Fasten off.

Starting from the edge

Cast on 80 stitches OR pick up 80 stitches OR work on the 80 stitches left after working sides.

Round 1: (k2tog, k8) to end (72 stitches).
Round 2 and all even-numbered rounds: k to end.
Round 3: (k2tog, k7) to end (64 stitches).
Round 5: (k2tog, k6) to end (56 stitches).
Round 7: (k2tog, k5) to end (48 stitches).
Round 9: (k2tog, k4) to end (40 stitches).
Round 11: (k2tog, k3) to end (32 stitches).
Round 13: (k2tog, k2) to end (24 stitches).
Round 15: (k2tog, k1) to end (16 stitches).

Break yarn and thread through remaining stitches. Fasten off tightly.

On straight needles

If you are not comfortable working in the round, work a top on two needles, then join the seam afterwards. If you do this with care, it should be almost invisible. Note that for tops worked on straight needles one extra stitch is added to the basic instructions for the seam.

Starting from the centre

Cast on 17 stitches.

Row 1: (k1, inc in next stitch) to last st; k1 (25 stitches).

Row 2 and all even-numbered rows: p to end.

Row 3: (k2, inc in next st) to last st; k1 (33 stitches).

Row 5: (k3, inc in next st) to last st; k1 (41 stitches).

Row 7: (k4, inc in next st) to last st; k1 (49 stitches).

Row 9: (k5, inc in next st) to last st; k1 (57 stitches).

Row 11: (k6, inc in next st) to last st; k1 (65 stitches).

Row 13: (k6, inc in next st) to last st; k1 (73 stitches).

Round 15: (k6, inc in next st) to last st, k1 (81 stitches).

Cast off, or leave the stitches on the needle ready to work the sides. Thread a length of yarn through the first 17 sts and draw up so the work sits flat with no hole.

Fasten off tightly.

Starting from the edge

Cast on 81 stitches OR pick up 81 stitches OR work on stitches left on the needle after completing the sides, increasing 1 stitch at the end of the previous row if necessary.

Row 1: k1; (k2tog, k8) to end (73 stitches).

Row 2 and every even-numbered row: p to end.

Round 3: k1; (k2tog, k7) to end (65 stitches).

Round 5: k1; (k2tog, k6) to end (57 stitches).

Round 7: k1; (k2tog, k5) to end (49 stitches).

Round 9: k1; (k2tog, k4) to end (41 stitches).

Round 11: k1; (k2tog, k3) to end (33 stitches).

Round 11: k1; (k2tog, k2) to end (25 stitches).

Round 13: k1; (k2tog, k1) to end (17 stitches).

Break yarn and thread through remaining stitches.

Fasten off tightly.

Tip

If the finished cover is slightly too large, do not despair! Thread a length of fine elastic (shirring or hat elastic is ideal) through the edge stitches on the wrong side of the work to pull it in. This is also effective if the lower edge begins to curl up.

Abbreviations
& Conversions

Abbreviations used in this book

BCr	back cross (slip next stitch to back on cable needle, k1, p1 from cable needle)
ch	chain
cm	centimetres
dc	double crochet
DK	double knit
dtr	double treble(s)
FCr	front cross (slip next stitch to front on cable needle, p1, k1 from cable needle)
foll	following
htr	half treble(s)
inc	increase by working twice into stitch
in(s)	inch(es)
k	knit
k2tog	knit two stitches together
LH	left-hand
p	purl
rem	remaining
rep	repeat
RH	right-hand
RS	right side of work
ss	slip stitch
st(s)	stitch(es)
tr	treble(s)
*	work instructions following * then repeat as directed
( )	repeat instructions inside brackets as directed
WS	wrong side of work

Yarn weights & terms

UK	US
Double knitting	Light worsted
Aran	Fisherman/Worsted
Double crochet	Single crochet
Cast off	Bind off
Tension	Gauge

Crochet hook conversion

UK	Metric	US
10	3.25mm	D/3
9	3.5mm	E/4
8	4mm	G/6

Knitting needle conversion

UK	Metric	US
9	3.75mm	5
8	4mm	6
7	4.5mm	7

Index

Contact us for a complete catalogue, or visit our website:
GMC Publications Ltd, 166 High Street, Lewes, East Sussex BN7 1XU, United Kingdom
Tel: 01273 488005 Fax: 01273 402866
www.gmcbooks.com